CLASSICAL INDIAN ETHICAL THOUGHT

CLASSICAL INDIAN ETHICAL THOUGHT

A Philosophical Study of Hindu, Jaina and Bauddha Morals

KEDAR NATH TIWARI

MOTILAL BANARSIDASS PUBLISHERS
PRIVATE LIMITED • DELHI

Reprint: Delhi, 2007
First Edition: Delhi, 1998

ISBN: 978-81-208-1607-7 (Cloth)
ISBN: 978-81-208-1608-4 (Paper)

MOTILAL BANARSIDASS
41 U.A. Bungalow Road, Jawahar Nagar, Delhi 110 007
8 Mahalaxmi Chamber, 22 Bhulabhai Desai Road, Mumbai 400 026
236, 9th Main III Block, Jayanagar, Bangalore 560 011
203 Royapettah High Road, Mylapore, Chennai 600 004
Sanas Plaza, 1302 Baji Rao Road, Pune 411 002
8 Camac Street, Kolkata 700 017
Ashok Rajpath, Patna 800 004
Chowk, Varanasi 221 001

Printed in India
BY JAINENDRA PRAKASH JAIN AT SHRI JAINENDRA PRESS,
A-45 NARAINA, PHASE-I, NEW DELHI 110 028
AND PUBLISHED BY NARENDRA PRAKASH JAIN FOR
MOTILAL BANARSIDASS PUBLISHERS PRIVATE LIMITED,
BUNGALOW ROAD, DELHI 110 007

Preface

Writing a book on traditional Indian ethics on which books are aplenty is by no means a novel enterprise. Yet, need for a book on the subject continues to be felt by students, research scholars and teachers of the universities to stimulate their thinking on newer interpretations. Books on the subject are often written in a historical perspective dealing with the ethics of the Vedas, the Upaniṣads, the Smṛtis and the philosophical systems in, more or less, a chronological manner. But that is hardly enough critical or philosophical to meet the need of the academic circle. The present work makes a sincere effort to fulfil that need.

Some books on the subject have been very ably written with a critical and philosophical insight. It is not therefore fair to complain that all books on the subject are of the same kind. Prof. S.K. Maitra's book *Ethics of the Hindus* may be cited as an example. The book is philosophical and critical, but it hardly takes any note of the magnificent developments that ethical thought has made in the present century, especially in the West. At the time Maitra's book was published these developments were perhaps not very well-known in our country. The present work takes full cognisance of the recent developments in the Western ethical thought and its likely impact on the understanding of the traditional Indian ethics. That is the speciality of the present work. Moreover, Maitra's book, as the title suggests, is a treatise specially on Hindu Ethics. Ethical ideas found in Buddhism and Jainism have been occasionally dealt with. On the contrary, the present work takes equal note of the ethical ideas contained in Hindu, Buddha and Jaina traditions, while dealing with the subject in its special framework of presentation.

The distinctive developments in Western ethics have given rise to certain well-knit conceptual moulds, which, if properly applied to any system of ethics, can help us to understand the subject better. That is what I have tried to do in my present book. In course of doing this, certain reconstructions were also made because material suited to these conceptual moulds are not always readily or directly available in the Indian thought. But to the best of my capacity, these reconstructions, have been kept legitimate limits so that they do not become jejune to the natural spirit of the Indian thought.

I have hope my present work will help scholars, teachers and student to understand the subject in a fresh light. If my hope in realised even partially, I will feel my labour to have been amply regarded.

In my work, I have got valuable help, in one form or the other, from some of my elders, colleagues and students. I am grateful to them. The first who comes to my mind is Professor Nityanand Mishra, Ex-Head of the Department of Philosophy, Bhagalpur University. It is he who actually initiated the idea of writing such a book and also encouraged me from time to time in my endeavour. I express my heartfelt gratitude to him. I am also indebted to late Professor R.K. Tripathi of Banaras Hindu University who enlightened me on my many intricate points. I am grateful to Dr. (Smt.) Pratima Ganguli, one of my best students and now my colleague for her many valuable suggestions. To many others who helped me in several ways I am grateful. Last, but not the least, I must thank M/S Motilal Banarsidass for readily taking up the publication of the work.

Bhagalpur, the 24th June, 1998 KEDAR NATH TIWARI

Contents

Abbreviations

1.	*RV*	*Ṛg Veda*
2.	*SB*	*Vedānta Sūtras, Śaṃkara Bhāṣya*
3.	*JS*	*Jaimini Sūtras*
4.	*SV*	*Ślokavārtika*
5.	*Bṛh*	*Bṛhatī*
6.	*VS*	*Vaiśeṣika Sūtras*
7.	*BG*	*Bhagavadgītā*
8.	*TV*	*Tantravārtika*
9.	*SN*	*Śukranīti*
10.	*Bṛh. Up.*	*Bṛhadāraṇyaka Upaniṣad*
11.	*Taitt. Up.*	*Taittirīya Upaniṣad*
12.	*RB*	*Vedānta Sūtras, Rāmānuja Bhāṣya*
13.	*NS*	*Nyāya Sūtra*
14.	*SS*	*Sāṃkhya Sūtra*
15.	*AV*	*Atharva Veda*
16.	*YV*	*Yajur Veda*
17.	*NB*	*Nyāya Bhāṣya (Vātsyāyana Bhāṣya* on *N.S.*)
18.	*Manu*	*Manusmṛti*
19.	*Āpastamba*	*Āpastamba Dharmasūtra*
20.	*Gautama*	*Gautama Dharma Sūtra*
21.	*Yājñavalkya*	*Yājñavalkya Smṛti*
22.	*Vasiṣṭha*	*Vasiṣṭha Dharma Sūtra*

CHAPTER I

Indian Concept of Morality

"What is 'morality'" is not an easy question to answer, although ordinarily it may appear to be so. As Frankena recognises, it is a "vague" and "ambiguous" question,[1] because, as W.D. Falk says, "'morality' has got 'multiple associations'" which are, according to him, "a bar to summing it up in any one way".[2] In a similar sceptical vein regarding the exact nature of morality, G.J. Warnock asks the question, "....is 'morality' clearly and sharply bounded?"[3] At least one ambiguity of the concept of morality is obvious. It is not very clear whether the question is about the nature of morality as it is distinguished from non-morality or immorality. Answering in the first sense will distinguish morality from other institutions of life such as religion, art etc. In this sense morality is an institution of life for any one to adopt in his life, so that his actions in terms of the moral point of view might be branded as good or bad, right or wrong, praiseworthy or blameful etc., or again he also may be entitled to judge others' actions as good or bad, right or wrong etc. In this sense 'morality' can be regarded as a particular way of looking at issues of character and conduct, which is not just any way (or point of view) but a particular way (or point of view). It is in this sense of morality that we talk of human beings as moral agents but not of animals. We also talk of moral concepts, moral laws, moral principles etc. Answering in the second sense, however, will make the term 'moral' more or less, synonymous with 'morally good' or 'morally right'. It is in this sense of 'morality' that we say that the essence of morality is compassion or the control of senses (*Indriyanigraha*) or something like that. Here 'being moral' does not mean adopting a particular point of view regarding issues of character and conduct, so that one may characterise them either as good or bad, rather it means 'being of a good character' or 'being of a good or right conduct' as contrasted with 'being of a bad character or conduct'.

1. Morality as Distinguished from Non-morality

Morality in the first sense may be taken in the Indian context as a general awareness or belief of man that human life by dint of certain specific elements involved in it has to observe certain principles of conduct and character. Morality means conscious living within the frame of certain principles of conduct laid down by those regarded as authorities. In general, therefore, the moral institution of life or the moral point of view consists in the awareness of an important distinction between what is and what ought to be. For man should live not merely in the light of what is but also what ought to be. To be more specific, it is the awareness of a living based on a distinction between our animal demands and the demands of the higher faculties of human life worthy of the distinctive nature of man. Traditional Indian thinking is mainly spiritualistic with a firm belief that man has a soul within him as his real being. This reality of soul sets for man a goal higher than any other goal to which our natural physical inclinations lead. So man has to adopt a point of view which helps him more towards the higher, spiritual plane, the plane of his real, inner being. Adopting the moral point of view therefore means adopting the really human point of view in which man finds it worthy of his inner nature to see himself as an agent. His actions may be evaluated as good or bad to set before himself certain principles of conduct so as to rise above the mere physical or animal aspect of his being. The moral point of view as distinguished from the non-moral point of view marks the recognition of man as a being of distinction. The Indian mind feels that morality as distinguished from non-morality marks the distinctness of man's nature and character. Consciousness of morality, as distinguished from non-morality, in man is that of his being a man whose actions may be branded as right or wrong on the basis of certain principles of conduct commensurate with his dignity and distinction.

In the West, generally speaking, the first sense of 'morality' (and naturally therefore the second sense also) carries with it, more or less, essentially a sense of social references. Outside a society there is no question of morality or moral point of view. The question of morality involves a necessary reference to some others in respect of whom one has to adopt a moral point of view or has to behave either in a morally good manner or bad manner. Kurt Baier, while answering the question what it is to adopt a moral point of view, holds that one adopts the moral point of view if (1) he is not being egoistic; (2) doing things on principle; (3) willing to universalize; and (4) in doing so takes into consideration the good of everyone alike.[4] Here we can see that the first and the fourth criteria have a necessary reference to others, to the members of a society or a group. Similarly, Frankena, while suggesting points for completing the list of criteria for an action-guide (judgement or principle) to represent a moral point of view, seems to be strongly inclined to add a fourth criterion also to the following three which he takes as purely formal:

(1) One takes it as prescriptive.
(2) One universalizes it.
(3) One regards it as definitive, final overriding, or supremely authoritative.

The fourth one that he adds to these three is as follows:

> It includes or consists of judgements that pronounce actions and agents to be right, wrong, good, bad etc., simply because of the effects they have on the feelings, interests, ideals etc., of other persons or centres of sentient experience, actual or hypothetical (or perhaps simply because of their effects on humanity, whether in his own person or in that of another). Here 'other' may mean 'some other' or 'all other'.[5]

Obviously, the fourth criterion makes morality or the moral point of view essentially attached to a social reference. Frankena is quite unambiguous in emphasizing the social reference of morality. He says, "Now, morality in the sense indicated (i.e., in the first sense) is, in one aspect at least, a social enterprise....it is an instrument of society as a whole for the guidance of individuals and smaller groups....Because of such facts, morality is sometimes defined as an instrument of society as a whole...."[6] According to Frankena, the moral rules and principles are social rules, and not ones which are spun by an individual. Again, they are applicable to an individual who lives in a society and who is expected to have certain obligations towards others. For a desert islander, perhaps, there is no question of morality. In short, morality worth the name may be called social morality, and not individual or personal morality. Moral point of view always refers to an individual in relation to a society and never to an individual in relation to himself.

In India the matter has been different. Morality may be both social and personal and sometimes the latter has been more emphasized. Morality as an institution of life has been recognized here from the very early age of the Vedas. Rather it has been recognized as the most basic element in human life. But then it has not necessarily been recognized as a social enterprise in the sense of being an instrument of the society to help guide the people living in a society. It is rather engrained in the very stuff or being of the universe. Man has simply to adopt it from there.

The Vedic cosmic principle of *Ṛta* is the foundation of morality. It gives the first indication to man for adopting a moral point of view. The *Ṛta* amongst other things implies that there is an eternal moral order involved in the very constitution of the universe and therefore man has to adopt a moral point of view. What *Ṛta* actually is and what various things it does imply we shall analyze and discuss in a later chapter. Here we have to see that as a principle of eternal moral order involved in the universe it gives man the first idea of morality. Thus morality as an institution of life or the moral point of view does not have its origin from a kind of social contract or from any such contingent agency. It is not a social enterprise or an instrument of the society for the guidance of individual conduct. It has in a sense a divine origin.

Although the *Ṛta* sometimes is characterized as an impersonal principle which also transcends the authority of the gods, it is more often seen working under the authority of some god like *Varuṇa*. *Varuṇa* is regarded as the custodian or the charioteer of the *Ṛta*, and in this sense morality may be taken as having a divine origin. In no case, however, morality has been taken here as a social enterprise. It has its origin in the scriptural references—the references as made in the Vedas and the Upaniṣads.

The Vedic distinction between *Ṛju* (straight) and *Vṛjan* (crooked) and the Upaniṣadic distinction between *Śreyaḥ* (desirable) and *Preyaḥ* (pleasurable) have much to do with the origin of the sense of right and wrong and hence of morality or the moral point of view in India. The *Ṛg Veda* contains a large number of passages illustrating the distinction between right and wrong, as straight and crooked, one of which may be cited here because of its poetic beauty:

> "The turbid darkness vanished, bright the sky shone, upward the light of Dawn, the heavenly, hastened, unto his fields on high the Sun ascended. The ways of mortals straight and crooked, seeing."[7]

The Upaniṣadic distinction between the desirable and the pleasurable is as follows:

> The desirable is one thing, and the pleasurable quite another. Both these, of different aim, bind a person.
> Of these two, well is it for him who takes the desirable.

He fails of his aim who chooses the pleasurable.[8]

The concept of '*dharma*' also, as it has been understood in the Indian tradition, owes much for the origin of the sense of morality. The term comes from the root '*dhṛ*' which means 'upholds' or 'supports'. So *dharma* is that which upholds the universe from within. And this *dharma* again in its broadest sense represents in the Indian tradition the moral law of the universe which regulates or governs the moral life of man. There is a belief in every Indian that it is the *dharma* or the moral law (or, in brief, morality) which upholds or sustains the universe. One has therefore to adopt the moral point of view i.e. one has to adopt the life of morality.

We can see that the moral point of view has its origin in the Indian mind not from contingent agency like society or some such thing, but it has a scriptural or divine origin. Furthermore, it is not the case here that a moral point of view has meaning only in the context of a society. In other words, the concept of morality is not necessarily tied up here with the concept of society. An individual may behave morally or immorally in relation to other members of his society as also in relation to himself. In other words, questions of morality will have to be faced as a member of society and as an individual. Even a desert-islander has to choose between a good and bad life, a moral and an immoral life. Man by virtue of being what he is has to follow certain obligations, even if he is not member of a society. There is talk of both social and individual morality in Indian ethics. It is more or less in this sense that writers like S.K. Maitra have talked of the presence of both objective and subjective ethics in India.

The objective or social ethic refers to questions of morality in relation to others, whereas the subjective or individual ethics refers to the questions of morality in relation to oneself. One is adopting a moral point of view not only in making judgements about the conduct and character of someone towards other members of the society, but also in his behaviour to himself as a man, when he lives far from any society.

Man, as distinguished from a brute, has to live a life worthy of a man. Even confined to himself he has to perform certain duties and inculcate certain traits of character. He has, for example, not to set his sense-organs free and unsaddled like the animals. He has rather to briddle and control them. In other words, he has to practise *indriyanigraha*, he has to undergo the process which leads to the purification of mind (*cittaśuddhi*). *Cittaśuddhi* is assumed to be an indispensable condition for the attainment of the higher values of human life. Man has to subordinate his lower impulses to the higher ones through a proper understanding of his inner nature and through the observance of some practical discipline. All these come, according to the Indian point of view, under the domain of morality. In other words, this individual or subjective process of discipline also constitutes a part of the moral life of man. This may be known as the individual or subjective morality because it is concerned with the discipline of one's inner being, one's mind or soul. According to Maitra, the psychological ethics of the Hindus includes "not merely the analysis of the will and its inner springs and their psychological as well as ethical classification, but also a part of their practical ethics as emboided in the various practical schemes of *cittaśuddhi* through external and internal aids."[9]

The recognition of both the objective and subjective morality constituting parts of the moral life of man corresponds to the acceptance of the morality of doing and the morality of being as part of the Indian concept. The morality of doing refers to the do's and don't's and the morality of being refers to the virtues and vices. Social morality is predominantly the morality of doing and individual morality is the morality of being. Inculcation of virtues and vices is basically a personal matter having reference to one's inner being and character, whereas social morality is mainly concerned with one's conduct i.e., with what one does or does not do in relation to the other members of his society. In one sense, it can be said that whereas social morality or objective ethics has its root in a sense of duty (towards others), individual morality or subjective ethics has its root in a sense of inculcating inner virtue.

It may be pointed out here that because the whole Indian scheme of moral life is directed towards the attainment of individual liberation (*Mokṣa*), it is more a repository of prudence than of morality. The sense of morality worth the name presupposes a sense of self-sacrifice for others. If what is done is ultimately for one's own sake, how can it be an example of morality? It cannot be anything other than prudence. This is more so in the case of what is called individual morality. For, social morality, even if it is ultimately directed towards the attainment of individual salvation, has at least outwardly a sense of duty or obligation towards others; it has a sense of the sacrifice of one's own interest for the benefit of others. But in case of individual morality, there is nothing like this, because it is plainly concerned with individual purification so as to make one's path for salvation clear. For example, *ahiṃsā, asteya, dāna,* compassion for others etc. have definite social implications in the sense that they are based on a consideration of one's fellow beings living in the society. But what can such practices as *āsana, prāṇāyāma* or other such means or *indriyanigraha* have bearings on others? Where is there in them any sense of the sacrifice of one's ego for the sake of others? How can these, therefore, be called moral or immoral?

Such objections against the Indian view of morality, we feel, are based on misunderstanding of the concept of morality in general and of self-sacrifice in particular. The institution of morality has for its basic concern the regulation of man's lower inclinations and promotion of the higher ones in realisation of his aspiration as a man. It is in such a concern that the transition from 'is' to 'ought' is involved. The natural inclinations of man go in favour of his own egoistic interest and therefore it is the concern of morality to instruct him to feel, think and do for others also. The sacrifice of one's egoistic interests does not always mean giving up one's own interest for the sake of others. It also means the sacrifice of lower interest for the sake of higher ones. The Hegelian maxim 'Die to live' does not mean only that one ought to sacrifice one's own interest for the sake of others, rather it also means that one ought to sacrifice one's lower sensuous interests in favour of the higher spiritual ones.

It is fact that man is generally inclined to do things in his own interest. Therefore, it may be true to say that the question of 'ought' or 'morality' arises only in the event of doing something for others. One must realise here that man is not inclined in a natural way to do all things in his own interest. He is inclined to do such things which promote his sensuous ends, and not those which lead to higher ends of life such as *Mokṣa.* So, self-sacrifice in the moral sense does not necessarily mean sacrificing one's interests for the sake of others. It may also result in sacrificing one's lower sensuous interests at the altar of the higher ones. So, questions of 'ought' also sometimes arise in relation to dispositions and actions which are in a broader sense in one's own interest. Kant spoke of the duties of self-preservation, the commitments which serve the interests of one's own rational being. Why? Why did Kant not hesitate to include such duties or commitments as one's moral duties along with the duties of social interest? The answer is: this is a concern towards which one ought to be reasonably inclined, but not naturally so inclined. So, the role of the institution of morality is not confined only to what is called social morality, it is also concerned with what in the Indian tradition is recognised as individual or subjective morality. W.D. Falk very rightly says, " 'Duty' and 'obligation' are not words unequivocally tied to the socially obligatory."[10] He further says in the same vein, "It is plainly not the principal function or nature of morality to protect the social 'order' if by the 'function' of a practice is meant the reason why it exists and is carried on....

Nor is the coincidence between ought-abiding living and the social interest axiomatic.... One may be conscientiously ought-abiding in serving one's community or in seeking personal salvation behind the walls of a Buddhist retreat."[11]

We may now try to understand in somewhat more precise terms Indian moral point of view in contrast with the Western one. By way of representing the Western point of view, Frankena puts down his position regarding the moral point of view in the following way: "My own position, then, is that one is taking the moral point of view if and only if (a) one is making normative judgement about actions, desires, dispositions, intentions, motives, persons, or traits of character; (b) one is willing to unversalize one's judgements; (c) one's reasons for one's judgements consist of facts about what the things judged do to the lives of sentient beings in terms of promoting or distributing non-moral good and evil; and (d) when the judgement is about oneself or one's own actions, reasons include such facts about what one's own actions and dispositions do to the lives of other sentient beings as such, if others are affected. One has a morality or moral action—guide only if and insofar as one makes normative judgements from this point of view and is guided by them.[12]

I think there should be no hesitation for anyone adopting a moral point of view even from the Indian standpoint if the four conditions as laid down by Frankena are followed by him. The first two conditions may be taken as universal, viz., (1) one is judging things normatively; and (2) one is willing to universalize. But the third and fourth may not be taken as necessary conditions from the Indian moral point of view. One may be adopting the moral point of view even if in judging some actions normatively, his reasons do not necessarily contain facts regarding the good or harm that the action does to others. The reasons may, on the other hand, contain only scriptural references either sanctioning or prohibiting the action, or else the reasons may contain facts regarding the regulation of the sensuous passions of an individual in favour of the higher spiritual attainments. In other words, from the Indian moral point of view, it is not necessary for an action, called moral or immoral, to have social implications and to lead to some good or evil in that reference.

2. Morality as Distinguished from Immorality

Let us now try to see the Indian concept of morality in the second sense of being morally right. In this sense it is not easy to define morality in contrast with immorality. What is 'morally right' or 'morally good' in the Indian tradition does not lend itself to clear understanding as a matter of definition. "As the dust that lies on earth, if pounded between two stones, becomes finer and finer, even so questions of morality, the more they are reflected upon become finer and finer."[13] That is, the more we proceed to ascertain the precise nature of morality, the more we are drawn into problems.

Perhaps this is why no serious effort has been made in the Indian tradition to understand the precise nature of morality, although a lot has been talked about various virtues, duties and obligations that men ought to inculcate or follow. In general, therefore, we can say that morality consists in inculcating certain virtues and doing certain duties while avoiding others. In other words, being moral means inculcating certain virtues and performing certain duties which ougtht to be inculcated or performed in virtue of one's being a man. But what virtues and duties are of this kind? Here, by and large, Indian tradition takes recourse to authority. In a way, it may be said that morality is defined in terms of authority. Whatever the Śāstras ordain to do is moral and what they prohibit is immoral. Morality therefore basically consists in following the dictate of the Śāstras (the Vedas, the Smṛtis etc.). As Śaṃkara says, "The holy writ is the ground of discriminating between right and wrong. 'This is duty', 'this is immorality'—all this can be known only by means of scriptures.... Śāstras alone constitute our basis for moral knowledge."[14]

'*Dharma*' in the Indian tradition may be broadly taken as equivalent to 'morality'. The equivalence is by no means perfect and unambiguous. As a matter of fact, '*dharma*', as used and understood in the Indian tradition, is a term of very wide connotation including within it the sense of a whole host of duties (as well as virtues) which ought to be performed by man. These duties do not always consist of acts ordinarily regarded as moral. Some may be seen as intellectual duties or duties relating to health or ritualistic duties or such other duties. For example, Manu while enumerating the ten *sādhāraṇa dharmas* of man also includes *śauca* (duty relating to health) and *vidyā* (Intellectual virtue or duty) within them. But then if one remembers that in India morality includes within it both social and individual morality, such virtues and duties which do not seem ordinarily to have a moral import, are so in relation to individual morality insofar as they contribute towards individual purification or self-control and self-elevation. Thus although the word '*dharma*' cannot be held synonymous with 'morality', the way how Indian thinkers have tried to define '*dharma*' will give us an idea as to what they understood by 'morality', or what it was for them to be moral as different from being immoral.

The famous Mīmāṃsā definition in this regard as given by Jaimini is as follows—"*codanā lakṣaṇo artho dharmaḥ.*"[15] This, according to Śabara's interpretation, means that whatever is indicated by the Vedic injuctions (or enjoined by the Vedas) and leads to the good is *dharma*. '*Codanā*' refers here to the injunctive text, '*Lakṣaṇo*' is that by which something is indicated. Thus '*codanā lakṣaṇo*' means what is indicated by the injunctive text. '*Artha*' means something conducive to good. Thus the entire *sūtra* means 'that which is indicated by the injunctive text and which leads to the good is *dharma*'. As a matter of fact, '*artha*' is a controversial term in the *sūtra* admitting of different interpretations. Śabara bases his above meaning on the distinction between *artha* and *anartha*. According to him, that which is conducive to *niḥśreyasa (yo niḥśreyasāya)* is *artha* and that which is conducive to *Pratyavaya (yo pratyavayāya)* is *anartha*. As a matter of fact, the Vedic texts in his view indicate both what is *artha* (i.e. what is good or moral) and what is *anartha* (i.e. what is evil or immoral). The *sūtra* has used the term '*artha*' only to preclude the possibility of acts which are not conducive to good, i.e., which are not moral. So *dharma* consists in following or obeying the injunctive texts which lead to good. The above definition, therefore, lays down two conditions for any act to be *dharma*—(1) it is enjoined by the Vedas and (2) it is conducive to good.

Kumārila, another commentator on the Mīmāṃsā sūtras, has certain differences with Śabara on the interpretation of the *codanā-sūtra*. There is hardly any essential difference so far as the general standpoint of the latter is concerned with regard to the nature of *dharma*. Insofar as the conditionalities for any action to be called *dharma* are concerned, both agree that the action must have behind it the authority of some Vedic injunction and that it should lead to the good. Where they differ is in the following.

The Vedic injunctions on which Mīmāṃsā lays stress by its above definition are concerned with ritualistic acts. According to Śabara's interpretation, the Vedic injunctions set forth rites like *Jyotiṣtoma*, which are *artha*, and like *Syena*, which are *anartha*. Kumārila would not like to agree with Śabara on this point. He took up the task of commenting on Mīmāṃsā sūtras in his *Ślokavārtika* a few centuries later. By that time the Vedas had come under severe attack in the name of *ahiṃsā*. It was felt that the rites like *Syena* propagated *hiṃsā*, which was evil. With a view to vindicating the moral perfection of the Vedas Kumārila tried to show that no Vedic rite in itself was *anartha* or evil. What was evil was its effect. Good or bad effect was not to be judged by reason. The Veda itself would decide what effect was good and what bad.

The Vedas abound in both injunctions and prohibitions. It is the prohibitions and not the injunctions which lead to evil consequences. If one tresspasses prohibitions, *anartha* is produced. So *artha* and *anartha* are the two opposite results emerging from the sacrifices—the former out of the injunctions and the latter when prohibitions are tresspassed. So killing of animals is not in itself bad. What is bad is its result and that will be decided by the Vedas themselves. As Kumārila says, "If however, the sinful character of the *Syena* belonged to its own form, then the subsequent passages (of the Vedas) such as '*hiṃsā ni sā*' etc. whould become incompatible."[16] So evil consequences, which are *anarthas*, are to be avoided but which are evil consequecnces need not to be decided independently by reason; the Vedas have decided them by means of prohibitions (*niṣedha*). As *Ślokavārtika* says, "For the comprehension of *Dharma* and *Adharma*, there is no other means save the fact of their being enjoined and prohibited."[17] With these points of view, Kumārila reformulates the definition of *dharma* as follows,—"That action alone is called '*Dharma*', which, even through its result, does not become tainted with sin, because such an action cannot but bring about happiness to the agent."[18]

Notwithstanding their differences regarding the nature of *artha* and *anartha* with reference to the Vedic rites, Śabara and Kumārila agree on what depends the *dharmatva* or morality of an action. It depends upon two things: (1) on its being enjoined by the Vedas and (2) on its leading to agreeable consequence. But Prabhākara, another interpreter of the Mīmāṃsā sūtras, does not at all seem to link the consequences of an action with the question of morality or immorality. For him *dharma* is that which is enjoined by the Vedas. The consequence does not come into picture while deciding the *dharmatva* of any action. He understands the *codanā-sūtra* in the following way, "*Dharma* is that which is enjoined by a Vedic injunction as to be effected by a qualified person." A qualified person is the one who comes under the sway of a particular injunction. Vedic injunctions and prohibitions appropriate qualifying titles to designate those who come under their sway. Such qualifying titles consist either in a particular desired object, or in a particular condition that affects a person, or in the case of prohibitions, in a partticular action that one is doing or about to do.[19]

Another important definition of *dharma* we find in the Indian tradition is of the Vaiśeṣikas: '*yato abhyudayaniḥśreyasasiddhiḥ sa dharmaḥ*'.[20] *Dharma* is that through which both (material) prosperity and highest good are achieved. Whatever is conductive to worldly prosperity as well as to highest good is *dharma,* according to the *Vaiśeṣikas.* Obviously, this concept of *dharma* or morality is necessarily teleological. Without reference to the teleos no action is either moral or immoral. If asked, what actions (or traits of character) lead to happiness and *niḥśreyasa,* the Vaiśeṣikas in general reply that they are laid down in the Vedas and the Śāstras. Of these actions (duties) some are common to all men, while some are specially meant for distinct castes and conditions. The common duties (or virtues) are the following: faith in *dharma,* harmlessness, benevolence, truthfulness, freedom from desire for possession, freedom from lust, purity of intention, absence of anger, bathing, use of purifying substances, devotion to deity, fasting and non-neglect (of duties).[21] Amongst the specific duties are the various *Varṇāśrama dharmas.* As regards the source of morality, we may see that reference to the Vedas and the Dharma Sūtras and Dharma Śāstras is made here also, but morality is not defined here in terms of what is enjoined in the Vedas, as is done by the Mīmāṃsakas. Morality is rather defined here with reference to the teleos, the goal that is achieved through its observance.

But if morality is defined in terms of the teleos or end that it leads to, what will happen to purely deontological notes as part of the Indian ethical tradition? One such example may be cited from *Mahābhārata,* where Yudhiṣṭhira tells Draupadī, "I act virtuously, O princes! not from the desire of reaping the fruits thereof, but of not transgressing the ordinances of the Veda, beholding the conduct of the good and the wise. My heart is naturally attracted toward virtue. The man who wisheth to reap the fruits or virtue is a trader in virtue. His nature is mean, and he should never be counted amongst the virtuous."[22]

On the whole, therefore, it can be said that 'morality' in the Indian tradition has been understood (rather defined) in terms of the mandates of the authority. This authority, for the most part, is contained in the Vedas, but, as we shall see in the next chapter on the sources of morality, the Smṛtis and the path trod by the "good" and the "wise" people also form such authority. Even Buddhism (and also Jainism) which does not believe in the authority of the Vedas and Smṛtis seems essentially tied up to an authoritarian concept of morality. The authority of the Buddha is final. Whatever conduct is prescribed by the authority for the regulation of either personal or social life is moral, not to follow it or to follow something other than it is immoral. In other words, it can be said that in the Indian tradition being moral means leading a principled or regulated mode of life both in the social and individual reference, the principle of regulation, however, coming mainly from authority. Morality in social reference means such acts and dispositions as love, compassion, charity, asteya, etc. and in individual reference all kinds of acts and dispositions related with self-control (control of the senses etc.), self-purification, self-discipline and self-elevation. Such acts may include the ritualistic acts, the acts regarding physical and mental purity such as *śauca, tapas, āsana, prāṇāyāma,* learning, wisdom etc. and such other acts.

Indian ethics being evolutionary in nature, concept of morality has undergone revision from time to time. The successive refinements through evolution has been detailed in a subsequent chapter. However, the supreme role of authority is nowhere denied in the Indian scheme of moral life, and morality always refers here both to social and personal obligations. The two distinguishing features of Indian concept of morality survive through the process of evolution: (1) Authority has the basis for deciding what is moral and what is immoral and (2) Morality refers not only to the social obligations but also to obligations related to one's own self.

REFERENCES

1. W.K. Frankena, 'The Concept of Morality' included in Pahel and Schiller's—(ed.) *Readings in Contemporary Ethical Theory* (Prentice Hall, Inc., Englewood Cliffs, New Jersey, 1970), p. 391.
2. W.D. Falk, 'Morality, Self and Others', included in Pahel and Schiller's (ed.) *op. cit.*, p. 390.
3. G.J. Warnock, *The Object of Morality* (Methuen and Co. Ltd. London, 1971) p. 1.
4. Kurt Baier, *The Moral Point of View* (New York: Random House, 1965), Chap. 5.
5. W.K. Frankena, *op. cit.*, pp. 391-92.
6. *Ibid.*, p. 6.
7. *RV* 4.ṛ.17
8. *Kaṭha Up*. 2.1.
9. S.K. Maitra, *Ethics of the Hindus* (University of Calcutta, 1963), p. 4.
10. W.D. Falk, *op. cit.*, p. 383.
11. *Ibid.*, p. 388.
12. W.K. Frankena, *Ethics* (Prentice Hall, Inc. Englewood Cliffs, New Jersy, 1973), p. 113.
13. *The Mahābhārata*, Śānti Parva, 136.11.
14. *SB* III.1.25
15. *JS* 1.22.
16. *SV* 218. (G.N. Jha's Trans.)

17. *Ibid.*, 242.
18. *Ibid.*, 268.69.
19. *Bṛh.*, pp. 110-111.
20. *VS* 1.2.
21. *Padārthadharmasaṃgraha* of Praśastapāda (G.N. Jha's Trans.), VI, II, 2, 3, 4, 5, 8 and 9.
22. *The Mahābhārata*, Vana Parva, 31.2-6.

CHAPTER II

Sources of Moral Ideas and Beliefs

1. Scriptures

As human beings we are advised to lead a moral life. Such advice comes from different quarters. But the question that comes to our mind: Where could we learn from the principles of morality—what to do and what to abstain from? Who will be our guide—our own conscience and reason or the advice and behaviour of other people or our ancient Śāstras and our old customs and traditions? In India, by and large, the authority of the scriptures, especially that of the Vedas, has been recognised to be the primary source of our moral ideas and beliefs. '*Vedo dharmamūlam*', says the *Gautama Dharmasūtra.*[1] After the Vedas, the authority of the Smṛtis is accepted in this respect (*tadvidām ca Smṛtiśile).*[2] In general, therefore, the Vedas and the Smṛtis taken together (of course, the former given the first preference) have been regarded as the source of morality. '*śruti smṛti vihito dharmaḥ*', says the Vaśiṣtha Dharmasūtra.[3]

However the above references do not seem to suggest that the Vedas and the Smṛtis are only our primary sources of morality, rather they seem to present the very definition of morality in terms of acts prescribed or approved by the Vedas and the Smṛtis. Only that is moral (as different from immoral) which the Vedas and the Smṛtis prescribe or approve of. The goodness or badness of our actions is to be ascertained only with reference to the Scriptures—the Śrutis and the Smṛtis. We have seen Śaṃkara saying in our first Chapter that Śāstras alone constitute our ground for discriminating between right and wrong. The *Bhagavadgītā* also takes the Śāstras to be the sole authority and guide in matters of morality. According to it, those who rely on sources other than the Śāstras for their guidance in matters of duties to be performed get happiness neither in this life nor in the life beyond.[4] Therefore, the *Gītā* specifically counsels to take the Śāstras and Śāstras alone as the final arbiter of right and wrong actions.[5]

In terms of what has been said above, Śāstras in general and the Vedas and the Smṛtis in particular emerge as the primary (rather only) sources of our moral ideas, beliefs and practices. It is not only that several references, as quoted above, emphasize the supreme role of the Śāstras in matters of morality, but also that several statements caution that a person who takes recourse to other sources of morality in lieu of the authority of the Śāstras, is liable to be regarded as immoral and punished. For example, the *Manusmṛti* says:

> "The Veda is called the Śruti and the Dharmaśāstra is called the Smṛti, their teachings should not be put to the test of logic, for virtue has emanated from these two."[6]

Again,

> "The Brahmin who tries to bring the Śāstras into contempt by dint of logic, shall be excommunicated from the society as a heretical caluminator of the Vedas."[7]

2. Path Trod by Great People

The prospect of a conflict among the Śāstras has been well-foreseen by the ancient Indian thinkers and some guidance is provided in the event of such an occurrence. The Mīmāṃsā gives a clear verdict that in the event of conflict between the dictates of the Vedas and the Smṛtis on any point, the former will prevail. The Smṛtis are to be regarded as authoritative only insofar as they do not transgress the authority of the Vedas. But, by and large, the Indian viewpoint in this regard seems to have been that in cases of conflict amongst the Śāstras, the path trod by great or pious people should be followed.

The *Manusmṛti* speaks of "*ācārascaiva sādhunām*" and "*sadācāra*" in this respect. The word '*sadācāra*', however, seems to have a reference to custom and tradition also, as may be seen from the following definition of *sadācāra* presented in the *Manusmṛti* "The tract of land which lies between the Saraswati and the Dṛsadwati, the two celestial rivers, that God-built country is known as 'Brahmavartam'. The conduct of life as it obtains from generation in that country amongst the twice-born and unmixed castes is known as *sadācāra*."[8] That custom and tradition should prevail in the event of conflict amongst the Śāstras is also clear from the statement of Manu, "In case of conflicting authority, let him take to the path adopted by his fathers and forefathers, by adopting that path he will not incur the enmity of any man."[9] But again the *Āpastamba Dharmasūtra* says that the rules of Śruti are more authentic and worthy of being observed than the customary or traditional courses of action (*śurutirhi balīyasyānumānikādācārāt*).[10] The *Mahābhārata* seems to be explicit in assigning a prominent role to the path trod by great people as a source of guide for our moral behaviour when it says, "Argument leads to no certain conclusion; the Śrutis are different from one another; there is not one *Ṛṣi* with infallible opinion; the truth about *dharma* or duty is hidden in caves; therefore that alone is the path which the great men have trod."[11] Thus the *Mahābhārata* seems to give, more or less, exclusive importance to the path trod by great people as our guide and source in matters of our moral practices. '*mahājano yena gataḥ sa panthāḥ*' is the ancient Indian saying in this regard.

But who are great people whose paths are to be followed? 'Great people' means morally good people, only the most refined souls. Manu has used the term '*Sādhu*' in this context to suggest that the path traversed by only people of the nature of sages is to be followed. A sage is known to have controlled all his passions and desires, who has no *kāma* and therefore in doing his work, he has no interest in the result. It is in this spirit that Jaimini says, "Those acts which cannot be ascribed to any worldly motive, and which are yet done by good men must be recognised as *dharma*."[12] Manu at one place seems to make his mind clear as to who is a good or pious man whose path is to be followed. According to him, such a man is well-versed in the Vedas and is free from attachment and aversion.[13] There is, of course, an apparent air of circularity in maintaining that in matters of morality the path adopted by good people should be followed. The question of people being good is a moral one and cannot be settled unless it is specified what kind of (moral) actions make people morally good. The general spirit behind the point is however clear and we have not much difficulty in deciding who are good people from the moral point of view. The Indian tradition repeatedly makes it clear that only such persons can set moral ideals for us who have won over the fire of passions, have no selfish motives, work only for the preservation and welfare of the society (*lokasaṃgraha* and *lokakalyāṇa*) and so on.

Sometimes the authority of the great or good people in guiding our action is accepted only half-heartedly. In the ultimate analysis the authority of the Śāstras prevails, as is evident from what Kumārila says in the *Tantravārtika*: "If the practices of good men are not in conflict with what is taught in the Veda and the Smṛti, such practices can be regarded as authoritative in matters relating to *dharma*, but when there is the least thing repugnant to the teaching of the Veda, then, as there would be a conflict of authorities, the practices can not be regarded as any authority at all."[14] The practice of good people is given importance, but such importançe is in subservience to that of the Vedas and the Smṛtis. Of these two also, the Vedas are regarded as superior. In the event of a conflict between the two, the verdict of the Vedas prevails.

3. The Voice of Conscience

While in matters of morality the authority of the scriptures and tradition set by the practices of good people play supreme role, conscience and reason are not wholly ignored. For example, Manu, besides taking the Veda, the Smṛti and the conduct of the saints as tests of morality, takes satisfaction of one's heart (*ātmatuṣti* or *svasya ca priyamātmanaḥ*) as the fourth test. This is very clear from his following two *ślokas*:

> *vedo'khilo dharmamūlam smṛtiśīle ca tadvidām*
> *ācāraścaiva sādhunāmātmanastuṣṭireva ca.*[15]
> *vedaḥ smṛtiḥ sadācāraḥ svasya ca priyamātmanaḥ*
> *etaccaturvidham prāhuḥ sākṣāddharmasya lakṣaṇam.*[16]

'*Ātmatuṣṭi*' in the first *śloka* and '*svasya ca priyamātmanaḥ*' in the second one seem to refer to the role of conscience in moral matters. Besides these, even in *śloka* II.1, where Manu seems to highlight the role of the practices of pious people in moral matters, he gives the "dictates of the heart" the ultimate position, as he takes them to be the concluding proof. Like Manu, Yājñavalkya also recognises the role of conscience as a source of morality when he says:

> *śrutiḥ smṛtiḥ sadācāraḥ svasya ca priyamātmanaḥ*
> *samyak saṁkalpajaḥ kāmo dharmamūlamidaṃ smṛtam.*[17]

Here we may mark that besides Śruti, Smṛti, *sadācāra* and inner conscience, Yājñavalkya also speaks of '*samyak saṃkalpajaḥ kāma*' as the source or test of morality. This means that even the desire arising out of right will or determination may serve as a source or guide to morality. But the main problem is to decide the right will. It may be said that the right will is the will of the pious or the good people and that way it need not form an additional test of morality; it may well be included under the third test as mentioned above, or else it may mean desire approved by conscience, and come under the fourth test as mentioned above.

That the dictates of inner conscience have been given an important place in matters of morality in the Indian tradition may be borne out by the general old saying '*manaḥ pūtam samācaret*'. Specially in such situations where several alternative paths seem to have their claims equally testified by recognised sources, the test of the inward satisfaction of heart plays the crucial role (*vikalpe ātmatuṣṭi ca*). The *Mahābhārata* lays down the following criterion in respect of the role of the inner conscience: "That code of morality which is honoured in every respect by those who are good, and which is approved by every honest heart should be followed."[18] Here, along with the example set by good people, the *Mahābhārata* takes the sanction of the heart to be an important aspect in deciding over moral matters. Several apt references to ancient Indian texts will corroborate the importance given to the voice of inner conscience in Indian tradition for deciding the question of morality in a specific situation. The ancient Indian viewpoint seems to be relying on the importance of the Śāstras as forming the source and guide of our moral ideas, beliefs and practices. In recent times, especially in the thoughts of Gandhi and Sri Aurobindo, conscience has been accorded a very important place as giving the final verdict regarding questions of morality and immorality. Sri Aurobindo states quite unambiguously: "There is only one rule for the ethical man: to stick to his principle of good, his intuition of good, his instinct of good, and to govern by that his conduct."[19] Similarly, Mahatma Gandhi, although so often declaring the *Bhagavadgītā* to be the principal source and guide of his actions, gives a very important place to the voice of his inner conscience. However, he cautions that any and every man should not be allowed to make morality a petty matter by taking the plea of the voice of his inner conscience. Only such persons have the right to act on the promptings of their conscience or intuition who have mastered over their selfish passions. In any case, however, personal intuition or conscience has not been denied its due place in Indian tradition as a source or guide of morality.

4. Reason

It seems, however, that reasoning or logic has hardly been given any recognisable place in the Indian ethical tradition. As we have seen, the very concept of morality (as contrasted from immorality) seems to be authority-based, and therefore, naturally, there can hardly be any place for reasoning. There are rather clear statements denouncing the role of reason in matters of morality. The two statements of Manu (II.10 and

II.11) quoted earlier in this very chapter clearly show that those who try to assess the opinions of the Vedas and the Smṛtis on the touchstone of logic and reasoning are to be despised and even excommunicated. Similarly, Kumārila, while emphasizing the place of the Śāstras (specially the Vedas) in matters of morlity, denounces the intrusion of logical reasoning in such matters. As he says, "For the comprehension of *dharma* and *adharma* there is no other means save the fact of their being enjoined and prohibited. Hence the introduction of an inferential argument is not proper."[20] Even the *Arthavāda* passages which apparently seem to be statements of reason are not regarded as such by the Mīmāṃsakas. It is said that instead of being statements of reason, they are statements of praise and commendation. Prabhākara says in this regard that the Vedic injunctions do not stand in any need of being supported by reason. They are self-valid and self-authorititive and therefore do not need any rational support.

However, the role of reason is not absolutely denied. Some role is assigned to it even by a thinker like Manu who apparently seems hardly giving any place to any factor other than the Vedas, the Smṛtis, the path of the good people and conscience (or intuition) in matters of morality, the first two, of course, being the primary in this regard. He rather allows a positive role to both perception and inference (or reasoning), besides authority, in giving us knowledge of the true principles of virtue. He allows even rational discussion of the teachings of the Vedas and the Smṛtis, provided the overall trend of the discussion is not hostile to the general tenets of these scriptures. This is very clear from his following *ślokas*:

> *pratyakṣaṃ cānumānaṃ ca śāstraṃ ca vividhāgamaṃ-*
> *trayaṃ suviditaṃ kāryaṃ dharmaśuddhimabhīpsatā.*
> *ārṣaṃ dharmopadeśaṃ ca vedaśāstrā'virodhinā*
> *yastarkeṇānusandhatte sa dharmaṃ veda netaraḥ.*[21]

That is, "he who wishes to know the true principles of virtue must know all the sciences which are based on positive observation, inference and the teachings of the Vedas. He who discusses the ethical teachings of the Vedas and the Smṛtis based on them by process of reasoning not hostile to their tenets is alone enabled to know the right principles of virtue and no one else." Similarly, in the following passage of the Śānti Parva, the *Mahābhārata* seems to assign some place to logical inference in matters of *dharma*, although the main role is assigned here to faith:

"The truths herein disclosed are incapable of being understood by inference alone or by that of mere study of scriptures. One must understand it by the aid of faith."[22] The citation is directly relevant for highlighting the role of faith. Indirectly it seems to be yielding a place to reasoning also. If inference alone is not considered sufficient for knowing the truths of morality, some role or relevance is conceded for inference in the case of morality.

A comparatively more respectable place has been accorded to reason in the Buddhist and Jaina traditions than in the Hindu. In these two traditions also, authority (of the Buddha and Mahāvīra) plays the most prominent roles as would be evident from several references and also from their general trend and spirit. For example, Mahāvīra is reported to have said: '*ānāyemāmagam dhammam*' (*Dharma* consists in following my commandments).[23] Similarly, in Buddhism, that the path laid down by the Buddha is to be followed strictly is evident from what the Buddha declared to his devoted disciple Ananda shortly before his *parinirvāṇa*: "I have expounded my doctrine throughout, in its entirety, Ananda; the Tathāgata has not the closed fist of a teacher who holds back something of his doctrine."[24]

Nowhere it is explicitly asserted that whatever the Buddha has said is the only moral and that alone is to be followed. The overall spirit sounds as if it were so. This is why Buddhism as a moral system has not generally been taken by its scholars as an autonomous system with personal reason having its full play. It is basically what may be called heteronomous, i.e., strictly based on the precepts and instructions of the Buddha. As S. Tachibana remarks in his book *The Ethics of Buddhism:* "Buddhists have many precepts which the Buddha laid down for the guidance of his immediate disciples, and many more which he delivered from time to time for the same purpose, both of which are embodied in the Pīṭaka. Whosoever professes faith in the Buddha has to observe and follow them. The Buddhist thus seems to be absolutely subject to external laws, in the form of precepts and instructions, and the Buddhist morality seems to be heteronomous, but not autonomous as it is generally understood to be."[25]

But despite the above, reason has been given a prestigeous place in both Jainism and Buddhism. In Jainism right faith is given the first place amongst the three jewels, yet the advice is not to proceed on blind faith. One is rather exhorted to use his own reason in ascertaining the validity and worth of the precepts before following them. Similarly, in Buddhism the path laid down by the Buddha is to be followed, the use of personal reason is neither disallowed nor despised. The four noble truths taught by the Buddha depict the basic truth and therefore they are to be followed, but reasoning or discussion on them is not disallowed. Buddha counsels that wherever there is disagreement, questions can be asked for removing doubts. As Buddha himself says while explaining his attitude in matters of morality to Kassapa, a nude saint, as follows: "......concerning those things in which we do not agree, let us leave them alone. For those in which we do agree let the wise put questions and ask reasons—discuss the matter either with their teachers or their followers."[26]

In modern Hindu thought, reason has been given comparatively better place, specially in the ideas of Vivekananda and Gandhi. For them also, however, reason is not the source of moral ideas. We can learn about morality from the Śāstras themselves. But if some precept or counsel apears contrary to reason, that is advised to be discarded. Gandhi is very clear and straightforward in his view in this regard. "I cannot let a scriptural text supersede my reason. Whilst I believe that the principal books are inspired, they suffer from a process of double distillation. Firstly, they come through a human prophet, and then through the commentaries of interpreters. Nothing in them comes from God directly....... I cannot surrender my reason while I subscribe to divine revelation."[27] Vivekananda's attitude in this regard may well be seen through is following lines: "I believe in reason, having seen enough of the evils of authority, for I was born in a country where people have gone to extremes in trusting authority."[28] And again, "It is better that mankind should become atheist through following reason than blindly believe in two hundred million gods on the authority of anybody.... The glory of man is that he is a thinking being."[29]

5. Conclusion

The above discussion makes it clear that the path followed by great people, one's conscience, intuition and reason have all played their roles in deciding the questions of morality and immorality in Indian tradition. The primary role is assigned to the Śāstras as the fundamental sources of morality. This is so because it is generally believed that various implications of morality can hardly be known fully through personal sources such as intuition, reason etc. The path trod by good people cannot always be a safe and sure guide because it is difficult to identify good people unless we know first what good is. In the *Mahābhārata* there are several passages which highlight the subtle and mysterious nature of morality. For instance, "It is difficult to find out the reasons on which duties stand even as it is difficult to find out the legs of a snake."[30] Also in Śānti, 136, the mysterious nature of morality has been emphasized. The relevant passage has already been quoted in Chapter I. It is because of this mysterious nature of morality that it is said in *Śukra-Nīti* "The theory of religion and morality is very complicated, hence people should practise the rules of Śruti, Smṛti and the Purāṇas, which have been followed by good people.[31] The passage gives out a clear indication of the reason why we should take recourse to the Śāstras in matters of morality.

The *Mahābhārata*, however, in virtue of the mysterious nature of morality, seems sceptical even about the Śāstras as giving us the final word regarding morality. The following long passage taken from the *Mahābhārata* will testify to it along with revealing the various complications and difficulties in deciding the questions of morality by any means whatever: "Thou sayest that righteousness or duty depends upon delicate considerations, that it is indicated by the conduct of those who are called good, that it is fraught with restraints and that its indications are also contained in the Vedas.....Duty and its reverse therefore cannot be ascertained by the study of the scriptures alone. The duties of a person who is well off are of one kind, those of a person who has fallen into distress are of another. How can duty be ascertained by reading the scriptures alone? The acts of the good, thou hast said, constitute duty. The good, however, are to be ascertained by their acts. The definition involoves, therefore, a begging of the question with the result that what is meant by the conduct of the good remains unsettled. It is seen that some ordinary person commits unrighteousness, while apparently achieving righteousness. Some extraordinary person may again be seen to achieve righteousness by committing acts that are apparently unrighteous. Again, it has been heard by us that the ordinances of the Vedas disappear gradually in the successive ages....when, therefore, all the declarations of the Vedas do not apply equally to all ages the saying that the declarations of the Vedas are true is only a popular from of speech which is indulged in for popular satisfaction. From the Śrutis have originated the Smṛtis whose scope again is very wide. If the Vedas be authority for everything, then authority would attach to the Smṛtis also, for the latter are based on the former. When, however, the Śrutis and the Smṛtis contradict each other, how can either be authoritative? Whether we know it or not, wherther we ascertain it or not, the course of duties is finer than the edge of the razor, and grosser than even a mountain.... One may thus see that all courses of conduct are seen to lose singleness of purpose and character."[32] *karmaṇo gahanā gatiḥ.*

REFERENCES

1. *Gautama* 1.1.1.
2. *Ibid.*, 1.1.2.
3. *Vasiṣṭha* 1.4.6.
4. *BG* XVI.23:
   yaḥ śāstravidhim utsṛjya vartate kāmakārataḥ
   na sa siddhim avāpnoti na sudhaṃ no parāṃ gatim.
5. *Ibid.*, XVI.24:
   tasmācchāstraṃ pramāṇaṃ te kāryākāryavyavasthitau
   jñātvā śāstravidhānoktaṃ karma kartum ihā'rhasi.
6. *Manu* II.10:
   śṛutistu vedo vijñeyo dharmaśāstraintu vai smṛtiḥ
   te sarvārtheṣvamīmāṃsye talehyam dharmo hi nirbabhau.
7. *Ibid.*, II.11:
   yo'vamanyeta te mūle hetuśāstrāśrayad dvijaḥ
   sa sādhubhirbahiṣkāryo nāstiko vedanindakaḥ.
8. *Ibid.*, II.17-18.
9. *Ibid.*, IV.78.
10. *Āpastamba*, 1.1.4.8
11. *The Mahābhārata*, Vana Parva, 314.119.
12. *JS* 1.3.7.
13. *Manu* II.1.
14. *TV* (G.N. Jha's trans.), 173-203.
15. *Manu* II.6.
16. *Ibid.*, II.12.
17. *Yājñavalkya* 1.7.
18. *The Mahābhārata*, Śānti Parva, 132.9.
19. Sri Aurobindo., *The Human Cycle*, p. 198.
20. *SV* 242-43.
21. *Manu* XII,105-106
22. *The Mahābhārata*, Śānti Parva, 252.13.
23. *Ācārañga Sūtra*, 1.6.2.180.
24. *Dialogues of the Buddha*, Part II, p. 107.
25. S. Tachibana, *The Ethics of Buddhism* (London, Curzon Press, 1926), p. 88.
26. *Dighanikāya*, Vol. 1.162
27. *Harijan*, Dec., 1936
28. Vivekanand, *Lectures on Practical Vedānta* (quoted by V.S. Narvane in his *Modern Indian Thought*, p. 94).
29. Vivekanand, *Essays on Jñāna-Yoga*, Complete works, Vol. II (quoted by V.S. Narvane in his *op. cit.*, p. 95).
30. *The Mahābhārata*, Śānti Parva, 132.19.
31. *SN* III.80.
32. *The Mahābhārata*, Śānti Parva, 266.

CHAPTER III

Object of Moral Evaluation

1. The Problem

Any voluntary action we perform has, generally speaking, two aspects —an internal and an external. The internal aspect consists in the motive or intention which prompts the action and the external aspect consists in the overt act performed or the result coming out of the action performed. Pronouncement of moral judgement upon someone's action has to be either on the overt act itself or on the inner motive that prompted the action. The problem is: on which of the two the moral judgement is to be passed?

There are various contingencies which call for resoultion of the problem. For example, let us suppose that a man throws a juvenile out of sheer fun with no intention to kill anybody, but the juvenile hits a man and kills him. Now, is the action of the man (his throwing of the juvenile and killing a person) to be judged as a wrong action? His intention was not bad, but the consequence of his action has been very bad. On what the moral judgement is to be passed—his intention or the real consequence? The question also relates to fixing responsibility of the action. Is the man throwing the juvenile with any bad intention or without? Conversely, actions prompted by evil motives may have brought about good consequences. Now, should such actions be called good because they have yielded good results? Or, should the actions be called evil because they were prompted by evil motives? Such questions have been extensively debated by Western moral philosophers. Indian thinkers have also not been indifferent to these. They seem to be rather quite alive to the aforesaid contingencies and have applied their minds to the solution of these. Both views find place amongst the Indian thinkers. The predominant note seems to be that right or wrong actions are to be judged in accordance with the good or bad intentions with which they are carried out. The overall Indian attitude seems to be one of reconciliation between the two factors. Each individual case is judged on its merit by weighing the relative importance of both the inner motive and the external consequence.

2. The Vedic View

A survey of the Indian thinking about the problem shows that the Vedas in general seem to teach an externalistic view of morality, where only acts performed are of any real significance. It is envisaged that whatever is done according to *Ṛta* or according to the will of gods is right, and all else is wrong. Right and wrong have no sanction of the inner character or motive, the simple sanction behind them is that of the gods. Sin is regarded simply as disobedience of the commands of a god like *Varuṇa*. One is free from sin not by changing his heart, his intention or motive, but by simply repeating rituals directed towards gods. The Vedas in general seem to give us an ethics of overt duties rather than inner virtues, an ethics of doing rather that of being, and all duties are clearly directed towards worldly ends, such as, health, length of life, offspring etc. Thus, on the whole, the Vedic view of morality seems to be externalistic, and it has little scope for the consideration of inner motive or intention of the doer for judging his act to be right or wrong.

3. The View of the Smṛtis

The Dharmaśāstras also preach an externalistic ethics where inner motive or intention of the doer does hardly seem to constitute the rightness or wrongness of the action done by him. Dharmaśāstras are more or less given to us in the form of a legal code. It is essential that the duties prescribed therein are to be followed. Sin does not lie in the defilement of the motive, but in either not doing the prescribed acts or doing what are forbidden. *Varṇāśrama dharmas* are to be followed quite mechanically. Mckenzie remarks about the morality of the Dharmaśāstras, and perhaps rightly, as follows:

> "............there has been represented in the Law Books anything but a very external view of life and conduct...... The emphasis has been on overt acts and not on the motives from which they have sprung. Sin has been feared as an evil substance that clings to one, bringing defilement, and its removal may be effected through physical means."[1]

However, it cannot be said that the Dharmaśāstras are destitute of any inner sense of morality. In spite of the overall air of externalism in the morality of the Dharmaśāstras, even Mckenzie admits that deeper in sights signifying the inner core of morality are evident at places. The Dharmaśāstras, of course, generally abound in external duties, but they also talk of inner virtues sometimes. Mere Actions carried out in a mechanical way without purity of heart and disposition do not bring the desired result. Gautama enumerates forty sacraments to be performed by each and everyone desiring release, but then he immediately adds eight finer virtues of the inner heart. He says that he whose soul is destitute of eight good qualities, will not be united with *Brahman* nor does he reach his heaven.[2] This is a clear indication towards the inner aspect of morality. Purity of motive and intention is also necessary for doing moral acts; only overt acts will not do.

4. The Upaniṣadic View

In the Upaniṣads and later in the *Bhagavadgītā* and other systems of Indian thought what is more important in ethical consideration is not the external acts, but the inner dispositions which prompt the acts. Sin is not merely failure to do the right, but failure to let good intention to act. Actions do not bind, what binds is the evil disposition. H. Lefever very rightly remarks about the connecption of sin as found in the Upaniṣads:

> "Sin according to this teaching is a question not of what one does, but of what one is. What stains, in other words, is not the action itself but root of the action....."[3]

5. Nyāya-Vaiśeṣika View

Almost all the Indian systems believe that our passions are at the root of all our actions. So actions are to be judged right or wrong in acordance with the good or evil passions which prompt them. According to the Nyāya Vaiśeṣika system, for example, righteousness and unrighteousness are the qualities of the self and not of the objective act which is prompted by the self. This is why it is the purity or impurity of our intentions (*abhisandhi*) which constitutes the rightness or wrongness of our actions. There is no merit or demerit in the action itself. It is always the intention which causes merit or demerit. Praśastapāda classifies spring of action into *icchā* and *dveṣa* (desire and aversion), both of which are mental dispositions which prompt actions. Vātsyāyana goes rather to an even deeper root '*moha*' from which spring *rāga* and *dveṣa*. The root of every action lies in the mind. True merit or demerit of an action, therefore, lies in the mind. If the act is born of a pure intention, it is good or right and if otherwise, it is bad or evil. There is no unintentional wrong in the strict moral sense. The intention is absolutely essential for constituting the rightness or wrongness of an action.

Śrīdhara, however, seems to be of opinion that even unintentional acts may be wrong, if they are proved to be examples of *pramāda* or carelessness. One may not have an intention to do wrong, but that is not enough. He must also take care of the fact that even in spite of his pure intention, his action in quetion may produce certain evil consequences. If he does not take proper care of the means and the likely evil consequences, he is to be blamed-for his action, not with reference to the intention, but the overt act performed and the result flowing therefrom.

6. The Mīmāṃsā View

The Mīmāṃsakas seem to hold that rightness and wrongness are objective categories and they have nothing to do with subjective motives or intentions. There are injunctions and prohibitions (*vidhis* and *niṣedhas*) in the Vedas and the question of rightness or wrongness pertains only to the carrying out of the *vidhis* and refraining from the *niṣedhas*. The rightness or wrongness thus consists only in the acts performed. If an action is in accordance with the Vedic injunction, it is right, and if otherwise, it is wrong. Even accidental acts, forbidden in scripture, are judged to be wrong and attract punishment in accordance with the law of *karma*. Thus, if a man kills a Brahmin even by pure accident he has to undergo the full penalty for that.

7. The Bauddha and Jaina Views

The Buddhist and the Jaina outlook on the question seems to be more or less similar to that of the Nyāya-Vaiśeṣika. Actions are good or bad not in terms of the external consequences they produce, but the inner motive which prompts them. In other words, it is the purity or impurity of motive which decides whether an action is right or wrong. If actions are judged in terms of their external consequences, it is argued, actions of saints who are indifferent to consequences of their action might be so branded, because they also produce the same consequences. But these acts are hardly judged as moral or immoral. They rather arise out of the subjective motives or intentions. The Buddhists also take *vāsanā* as the root cause of all actions, and hence moral judgement is to be passed on the good or evil *vāsanās*, which are the sources of our actions, and not upon actions themselves.

However, neither Buddhism nor Jainism fully ignores the importance of consequences in judging an action to be right or wrong. Their attitude seems to be that only consequence does not determine the rightness or wrongness of an action. The Jaina view seems to bring about a synthesis between the consequences and internal motives in of an action. As professor S.K. Maitra remarks with regard to Jainism in a relevant context: "Hence we have here a synthesis of externalistic, consequential morality with the internalism of the theory of self-determination. While the consequence by itself does not determine virtue or the opposite, it furnishes the content as it were in relation to which the subject has to determine itself in the direction of righteousness or unrighteousness."[4] Similarly, the Buddhists also do not seem to take consequences totally out of consideration while judging an action good or bad.

That consequences also play an important role according to the Buddhists in contributing to the morality or immorality is evident from their views on institutional morality. The idea of institutional morality entails that the founder of an institution is responsible not only for the consequences he intended to flow from the activities of the institution but also for all the intended or unintended later consequences to flow from the activities of the institution. For example, if a man establishes a shrine to provide temporary shelter to the pilgrims, but later on after his death the shrine is converted into a place of illegal traffic, the founder of the institution is to be held responsible for all such immoral acts. The act of founding the institution by the founder may be characterised as an immoral act in view of the consequences that flow from it, notwithstanding the good intention of his founding it. The founder, according to this view, should have perhaps foreseen all the likely consequences that might emerge from the founding of the institution even in future.

The inner motive and the external consequences have received appropriate emphasis in Indian tradition of moral evaluation. While some systems have emphasized upon the role of inner motives, others have upheld the role of external consequences, the overall atmosphere remaining one of reconciliation, i.e., of recognising the role of both. The *Mahābhārata* on the whole gives primary importance to the prompting motive or intention, but in certain specific cases where the relative merit of actions is to be judged, reference to their consequences becomes inevitable. When, for instance, Yudhiṣṭhira enquires from the snake, "Which, O snake!, is the right of the two—truth or alms giving?", the snake replies, "The relative merit of these virtues—truth, alms giving, kind speech and abstention from injury—are known by their objective utility. Even so it is, O king! depending on effects."[5]

REFERENCES

1. John Mckenzie, *Hindu Ethics* (Oriental Book Reprint Corporation, New Delhi, 1971), p. 64.
2. *Gautama* 1.8, 24.
3. H. Lefever, *The Vedic Idea of Sin* (London Mission Press, Nagarcoil, Travancore, 1935), p. 84.
4. S.K. Maitra *op. cit.*, p. 219.
5. The *Mahābhārata*, Vana Parva, 183, 3-7.

CHAPTER IV

Characteristics of Indian Moral System

Indian philosophy has its own distinctive characteristics in contrast with those of the Western philosophy. Indian moral system or Indian ethics also has certain characteristics which are its own. As a matter of fact, in India a sharp distinction has hardly ever been drawn between philosophy, ethics and religion. The three have been pursued together. Mokṣa has been regarded as the end of life and all the three pursuits—philosophical, ethical or religious—are ultimately meant for the attainment of that goal. Philosophy is as much a means to Mokṣa as ethics or religion is. All the three proceed together. Philosophy intermingles with ethics and religion and vice versa.

What is called philosophy, or more properly Darśanaśāstra in the Indian context, is not merely a field of intellectual or rational discussion for knowing or understanding the nature of the fundamental reality; it is also, and perhaps more prominently, a practical guide for spelling out the nature and means of liberation. All sorts of philosophical discussions—metaphysical, epistemological, logical, linguistic—are there, but they are all fundamentally oriented towards the above noted purpose. And ethics and religion are rather more naturally disposed towards that goal.

A recognised boundary between the three domains has hardly been drawn traditionally. This is why many Western thinkers have been reluctant to admit the existence of ethics or philosophy in India in the true sense of the terms. According to them, there is only religion here. But this is all very clearly a prejudice. As already noted above, philosophy, ethics and religion have remained intermingled here. But on the conceptual level a distinction between the three may very well be made. There is a full-fledged moral system here with some very distinctive characteristics of its own. Let us see these characteristics at some length.

1. Social and Individual Ethics

Indian moral system contains within it both social ethics and individual ethics. We need not elaborate this feature of Indian ethics here because we bave already referred to it in detail in our very first chapter on Indian concept of morality. The whole of Indian moral system proceeds on the assumption that as a human being every man has to discharge two types of moral obligations—one related to the other members of the society and the other related to one's own self. Under the former come such virtues or duties as *ahiṃsā, dāna, dayā* (compassion) *paropakāra* (help or service to other), *asteya* (non-stealing of the property of others) etc., while under the latter come *indriya-nigraha* (control of senses), *aparigraha* (non-attachment to worldly objects), study of the scriptures, *śauca* (cleanliness), *āsana, prāṇāyāma* and such other methods of *cittaśuddhi* etc. The idea here is that morality is the inculcation and practice of characteristic human virtues as against the animal inclinations. The question of the inculcation or practice of such human virtues or duties arises not only in relation to the other members of the society, but in relation to oneself also by virtue of one being a man, and not a bare animal.

2. Spiritualistic Outlook

By and large, Indian moral system may be said to be based on a spiritualistic outlook with regard to the universe. One is to be moral here not simply on certain rational considerations. It is because of one's spiritual nature that every man is obliged to be moral both in the sense of social and individual morality. Everyone shares the same spiritual foundation, and therefore there is no question of enmity with any other. Virtues like love, kindness, self-sacrifice, non-stealing etc., become natural for everyone to inculcate and observe. Each individual is spiritual in nature by virtue of having a soul within as his essential being. He has to control and regulate the demands of his lower being for the sake of the higher or the spiritual. Hence, the virtues of self-control, control of the senses, non-attachment to worldly objects etc. which form the elements of individual morality, come as a matter of necessary consequence.

Indian outlook is spiritual and the Indian moral system is oriented towards that spiritual goal. The spiritual goal is generally known as *Mokṣa* and morality in any of its form is a means to that goal. So morality in India is thoroughly spiritualistic. There is one materialistic system of thought also in the Indian tradition which neither believes in the spiritual foundation of the world nor in a spiritual goal. But the tone of the system proves to be so meagre in the overall spiritualistic atmosphere, that it has hardly any impact on the Indian moral system.

3. Metaphysical Basis

Indian moral system has a metaphysical basis. In the West, ethics is autonomous and it does not need to have a metaphysical or religious foundation. It is a social affair and therefore the ought-questions of morality are to be decided simply on social and rational considerations. It does not need to have any transcendental basis. Moreover, metaphysics purports to deal with factual (although of a fundamental nature) questions and purely factual considerations can never become a foundation for deciding ought-questions. For, from mere 'is', there is no passage to 'ought'. If, however, we make such a passage, we become victim of a fallacy popularly known as 'naturalistic fallacy'.

But in India, the matter has been different. Here, it has been felt that morality must have a metaphysical or religious foundation, otherwise it would be rootless, shallow, non-serious and artificial. As Dr. Radhakrishnan says, "Any eithical theory must be grounded in metaphysics, in a philosophical conception of the relation between human conduct and ultimate reality. As we think ultimate reality to be, so we behave. Vision and action go together."[1] In a way the very second characteristic mentioned above shows that Indian moral system has got a metaphysical basis. Spiritualism itself is a kind of metaphysics and is the very core of religion.

That Indian moral system is spiritualistic in the above sense implies that it is based on metaphysics. Even the hedonistic Cārvāka ethics is based on its materialistic metaphysics. Any moral system to be sound and significant must have a sound metaphysical system at the back of it. Ethical principles may not be logically derivable from the factual premises to which a particular metaphysics gives rise, but the former is "contextually implied" by the latter. 'The same soul identical with the fundamental reality *Brahman* is present in every human being' may be true as a metaphysical premise but the moral principle 'No one ought to injure any other' or 'we ought to love each other' does not follow from it logically. Nevertheless, it is undeniable that the former provides a good reason for the latter.

4. Authority as the Primary Source

Authority is the primary source of Indian ethics. This point has been elaborately dealt with in Chapter II and therefore it need not be explained at length here. However, certain general points may be discussed here. Indian thinkers had in their minds morality as a universal human pursuit which could not be left to personal whims and decisions of any and every one. We have seen morality recognised as a very complicated and delicate affair. If it is to be something continuously worth pursuing for elevating man's life, it must be left to those few men of vision, who have gone through various aspects of human life and can foresee the situations to which human beings are exposed. This can be expected only from the great *ṛṣis*, the authors of the Śāstras. This is why great *ṛṣis* or *ṛṣi*-like people in all ages are respected and followed. In the main, however, Śāstras remain the foundational source of morality not only in the eyes of traditional Indian thinkers but also in the eyes of most or almost all the contemporary Indian thinkers.

5. More Preceptive than Speculative

Indian ethics has been more preceptive than speculative or critical. Indian thinkers have always adopted a practical outlook and consequently they have never separated theoretical thinking from their practical consequences. This is obvious in Indian philosophical thinking conspicuously marked, as it is, by the practical concern of liberating people from the ocean of worldly misery. Even in logical thinking this concern may be seen in the Indian logician's refusal to bring about sharp distinction between formal and material truth or between deduction and induction. This concern finds articulation in Indian ethics which is by and large preceptive, prescriptive or normative. In other words, the primary concern of Indian ethics has been to prescribe norms for a morally elevated life in both its personal and social aspects.

It has hardly concerned itself with theoretical discussions regarding problems of ethics. In other words, Indian ethics for the most part has been a system of moral principles, moral codes or moral precepts which are directly concerned with regulating man's life to higher spiritual ends. It cannot be called moral philosophy. This is all the more true about the ancient Indian ethics in comparison with the contemporary one. In any case, it has not been a field of pure analysis of ethical terms, judgements, arguments etc. as it has been in the West recently. Undoubtedly, Indian ethics does not lack in the analysis and elaboration of the meanings of some of the key terms such as *niḥśreyasa, puruṣārtha, dharma, pravṛtti, niṣkāma karma* etc. and the related psychological terms such as *preraṇā* (motive), *abhisandhi* (intention), *rāga* (attachment), *dveṣa* (aversion) etc., but then it does not involve itselt in such analysis for the sake of analysis itself. Its main concern has always remained making the ethical norms more precise, more elaborate etc. so that they may guide each and every aspect of human life. In brief, Indian ethical pursuit has hardly ever been a purely meta-ethical pursuit, although, as we shall see later, elements of meta-ethics are present in it and an Indian meta-ethics may well be reconstructed. Moreover, because the chief concern of the Indian thinkers has been to make human life morally and spiritually motivated, they have stayed away by and large from critical discussions about moral problems. Authority has been their chief guide in moral matters and it has been stressed upon that the dictates of the authority should be observed and followed in matters of morality, more or less, ungrudgingly and uncritically

6. Humanism

Indian moral system is out and out humanistic. To many Western readers, this characteristic may sound just the opposite of what they have so far thought to be the actual position. Many Western thinkers dealing with the ethical aspect of Indian thought have opined that room for humanistic ethics in Indian thought is unlikely, because it is basically other worldly and life-negating in its approach. Such an impression about Indian thought betrays one's utter ignorance about its true nature and spirit. Dr. Radhakrishnan has clearly demonstrated it in his book *Eastern Religions and Western Thought* by way of answering to the charges levelled against the Indian thought by Dr. Schweitzer. The latter's charges are directed against the Advaitic standpoint of Śaṃkara. The charge can be countered by saying that Śaṃkara's Vadānta does not constitute the whole of Indian philosophy. Moreover, even if it is deemed to be presenting the essential spirit of Indian thought, the charge levelled by Dr. Schweitzer against it hardly stands in the light of a correct and clear understanding of the Vedāntic position.

The Advaita Vedānta does not deny the reality of this world outright. Rather, on the contrary, it fully affirms the reality of the world from the practical standpoint. And from this standpoint all ordinary human relationships are fully real, so that there is a full-fledged scope for a humanistic ethics. Even from the real standpoint, or what may even be called the transcendental standpoint, Śaṃkara does not so much deny the reality of this world as he insists on re-interpreting it. According to him, what is to be realised from the real standpoint is not that the world is complete void, but that it is fully spiritual and devoid of multiplicity. The multiplicity and materiality are illusions. What is real is spiritual unity. And what can be a more solid basis for humanistic ethics, rather for a universalistic ethics, than this kind of realisation that the apparent multiplicity of the world is sheer illusion and what is real is a basic spiritual unity? This will be still clearer if we try to see to some extent what humanism actually means and implies.

As a matter of fact, 'humanism' is a term which has a very wide connotation and therefore it may not be very easy to define it in a precise manner. Nevertheless, there are a few elements which are taken to be essentially involved in it. The first and the basic principle of humanism seems to be that man is the crown of the universe, that in nature nothing is higher than him. And by 'man' is meant here not the abstract man, the man as a species, but each individual man in his own independent capacity. This leads us to the second point that man is his own goal and that he has to attain no goal other than or ulterior to himself. To attain one's own perfection, to realise the maximum potentialities implied in oneself is man's end. And thirdly, in the realisation of this goal each man is to serve as a supporting hand, a helping hand, for every other fellow being. Consequently, humanism fosters virtues like mutual brotherhood, love, compassion etc. as essential elements of any moral system.

Now, Indian philosophy in general and Indain moral system in particular, based on a spiritualistic metaphysics, demonstrate that the essential elements of humanism are present herein in a far deeper way than in the Western tradition. In Indian thought, man is regarded as the highest in creation not because he is rational or has the highest intellect to achieve wonders, but because he is spiritual in nature. In Western concept of humanism these empirical or positivistic considerations may be taken as the characteristic features of the highest status for man but Indian thought gives man such a status because of a soul or spirit in him which is his essence and because of which man is really the divine. In the nature of his soul, man shares the basic reality *Brahman* or God himself. According to the theists like Rāmānuja and others, the soul in man is God's spark in him. Thus man is essentially divine. For those systems which are apparently atheistic, man is the highest in the capacity of his soul, because this soul is capable of attaining infinite possibilities. As Jainism says, it is capable of attaining *ananta catuṣṭaya*—infinite faith, infinite power, infinite knowledge and infinite bliss. Thus, man being himself essentially the divine is the highest. Tagore in contemporary Indian thought has emphasized this inner divine and infinite nature of man the most.

About the goal of man's life, right from the age of the Upaniṣads, emphasis has been on self-realisation or self-perfection or self-knowledge (*ātmānam viddhiḥ*) in Indian thought. No goal higher than man's own perfection, realisation of one's own soul, has been recognised here. As a matter of fact, all moral pursuits are ultimately meant for this goal. In the ladder of gradual upliftment, social morality gives way to individual morality of *indriyanigraha* and *cittaśuddhi* which, through other higher means, leads to the ultimate end of self-realisation. And the humanistic virtues of compassion, love, brotherhood etc. become a matter of automatic consequence of the Indian concept of man outlined above. Because each man shares the same divine in the nature of his soul, so all are essentially one and the same. Where is the scope for hatred, enmity etc. between one another then? Love and compassion for each other becomes the automatic result. Dr. Radhakrishnan very rightly points out that in Christianity it is said 'Love thy neighbour as thyself', but if somebody asks the question, 'why'?, perhaps Christianity does not have within it any worthwhile reply. The reply is there in Hinduism: 'Because everyone of us shares the same divine essence in the nature of our soul', or, in brief, 'because between oneself and one's neighbour there is no essential difference'. Dr. Paul Deussen, the great Indologist, has sounded this note very beautifully and straightforwardly in the following words that he uttered to a gathering at Bombay at the end of his Indian tour, "The Gospels quite correctly establish as the highest law of morality, 'Love your neighbour as yourselves'. But why should I do so since by the order of nature I feel pain and pleasure only in myself, not in my neighbour? The answer is not in the Bible....but it is in the Veda, in the great formula 'That art Thou' which gives in three words the combined sum of metaphysics and morals. You shall love your neighbour as yourself because you are your neighbour."[2] And this shows that the Indian ethical system is not only humanistic, rather its humanism has a sound metaphysical (spiritual) basis that gives it depth of significance.

7. *Mokṣa* as the Ideal of Life

Morality by itself has not been given the highest status in India; the ideal of life is *Mokṣa*. The point is very clearly vindicated in the Indian theory of *puruṣārthas*. There are four *puruṣārthas—Kāma, artha, dharma* and *Mokṣa*, of which the last one is the highest. The three earlier *puruṣārthas* in the order they are mentioned do not however represent the progressive steps of the ladder such that *kāma* comes first, then *artha* and then *dharma*. As a matter of fact, *dharma* pervades both *kāma* and *artha* such that in the observance of both of them *dharma* must be our essential guide. So, *dharma* has been given a pervasive status, but not the highest status. Even those who advise the observance of *dharma* for its own sake, do not take *dharma* as the highest ideal. The highest ideal for them also is *Mokṣa*. For example, the *Mahābhārata* in general and the *Bhagavadgītā* in particular as well as the Prabhākara Mīmāṃsā take the observance of *dharma* as essential not for the sake of some ulterior end but for its own sake. They seem to preach in their own ways what may be called a doctrine of *dharma* for the sake of *dharma* or duty for the sake of the duty. But they also regard *Mokṣa* as the highest ideal of life.

Is then *dharma* a means to *Mokṣa?* No straight answer can be given to this question. Different views are held by different system of Indian thought in this regard. The Sāṃkhya, the Advaita Vedānta and, in more recent times, Sri Aurobindo do not take morality necessary for the attainment of *Mokṣa.* Those systems which take morality as a necessity for the attainment of *Mokṣa*, hardly regard it as sufficient for the purpose. Its role is simply recognised as something which paves the way for *Mokṣa* to some extent and then melts away in oblivion to make room fot other more effective means for the purpose. This makes John Mckenzie remark as follows: ".....*dharma* has to do with a lower sphere of experience. It serves as a sort of platform over which one may climb to a position from which it becomes easier to reach the higher, but when this position has been reached it is no longer needed.[3] Mckenzie's remark, however, comes by way of criticising Indian view of morality with a view to belittle its importance, but with that kind of attitude we do not agree. If morality is not given the ultimate status in favour of some more effective means of *Mokṣa,* that cannot in any way be a point with reference to which we may belittle the importance of morality in Indian view. Indian thinkers have their reason to believe why morality cannot be a direct means to *Mokṣa* and it must be forsaken after a certain stage in favour of some more relevant means. It is perhaps felt that *Mokṣa* is a different category altogether, which requires self-knowledge, self-realisation. And this can be possible only in an intuitive flash through some sort of spiritual concentration or *yoga.* Moral actions, howsoever efficient they may be in making our wordly life happier, cannot give us the type of realisation *Mokṣa* requires. As Radhakrishnan says, "While ethical life can give rise to a better existence, it by itself cannot in effect realise, which requires the shifting of the very basis of all life and activity."[4] Or again, "*Jñāna,* or seeing through the veil of *māyā,* is the spiritual destiny of man. It is something more than ethical goodness, though it cannot be achieved without it.....One is an improvement of human nature, while the other is reorientation of it. We cannot reach perfection by means of progress any more than we can reach the point where the clouds touch the horizon by running:"[5] In a, more or less, similar vein, Sri Aurobindo writes, "Ethical conduct is not the whole of life; even to say that it is three-fourths of life is to indulge in a very doubtful mathematics. We cannot assign to it its position in any definite language, but can at least say that the kernel of will, character and self-discipline are almost the first condition of human self-perfection."[6] All these clearly show the insufficiency of morality in leading us to the highest ideal due to the specific and unique nature of the latter. But that does not in any way minimise the importance of morality insofar as it goes.

Why morality has not been regarded as a direct (or sufficient) means to *Mokṣa* by the Indian thinkers is perhaps due to their belief that *karma*, good or bad, binds. Good (or moral) actions lead to good rebirth, but rebirth itself is bondage. So, to get complete release from the fetters of bondage we are ultimately to rise above the level of *karma*, and hence of morality of *dharma*. Actions are required to be carried out without attachment to results. Rather, all Indian systems advocate performance of such actions. Only such actions which are done with a sense of attachment bind us. So, non-attached actions are to be performed, because no binding *saṃskāras* are generated out of them. *Niṣkāma karmas* (non-attached actions) are like fried seeds which do not germinate. So, what is advised to be given up is not action, but action done with attachment. At no level actions are to be given up. Moral actions in the sense of *niṣkāma karmas* have rather liberating effects. The Mīmāṃsakas advise performance of *nityanaimittika karmas* (which may very properly be deemed as *niṣkāma karmas*) up to the final stage of liberation. According to them such actions are not to be given up any stage. Whether all *niṣkāma karmas* are moral actions is a different question which we shall take up at a later stage. In a sense, these *karmas* may be regarded as morally neutral, but taking them in the actual spirit they may be seen to be morally relevant and important.

Modern Indian thinkers such as, Vivekananda, Tagore and Gandhi, have sought to make morality a direct means to *Mokṣa*. They present such a conception of *Mokṣa* that even social morality by itself becomes directly relevant for the attainment of *Mokṣa*. *Mokṣa* for them is nothing other than what Tagore specifically calls realising oneself into others and others into oneself, or else, realising the universal self within the individual self. Such a realisation, they point out, perhaps rightly, is possible only by cultivating the social virtues of compassion, love, brotherhood etc. Morality becomes a path of direct relevance for the attainment of the highest ideal of life. In the light of what man can possibly attain by way of realisation, Mckenzie's remark proves to be totally misconceived and mistaken.

REFERENCES

1. S. Radhakrishnan, *Eastern Religions and Western Thought* (Oxford, Clarendon Press, 1940), p. 80.
2. Quoted by Radhakrishnan in his *op. cit.*, pp. 101-2.
3. John Mckenzie, *op. cit.*, p. 207.
4. S. Radhakrishnan, *op. cit.*, p. 103.
5. *Ibid.*, p. 94.
6. Sri Aurobindo, *op. cit.*, p. 131.

CHAPTER V

Basic Presuppositions of Morality

1. Freedom

In saying, as we often do, that one ought to do this and ought not to do that or this is right and that is wrong, there is a presupposition that everyone can act in his own right, by his own free will. For, if he has no such capacity or power, it is futile, or even senseless, to exhort or advise him. In India, morality is looked upon as primarily based on the authority of the Śāstras. The Śāstras prescribe a lot of do's and don'ts for all persons or for specific category of persons. But what would all these injunctions and prohibitions mean if the concerned person had no capacity or power or will of his own to follow the prohibitions and injunctions? Moreover, the Śāstras on many occasions provide for various rewards and punishments for the right doers and the wrong doers respectively, but what could such rewards and punishments mean if the doer could not be held personally responsible for what he did? Responsibility clearly implies free will. Free will then seems to be the very basis, the fundamental presupposition behind any talk of morality.

Indian ethics also does not seem indifferent or deaf to this basic presupposition of morality. This seems very clear from the following lines of the *Mahābhārata*: "If a person were not, in the matter of his acts, himself the cause thereof, then, sacrifices would not bear any fruits in his case, nor would anybody be a disciple or a master. It is because a person is himself the cause of his work that he is applauded when he achieveth success, and censured if he fails. If a man were not the cause of his acts, how would all this be justified?"[1] Again, in reply to those who take Time or *Kāla* or Destiny to be everything in our acts to such length that whatever we do, we do under the dictates of the *Kāla* and we have no freedom of our own, it has been said, "If it is Time that causes weal and woe and birth and death, why do physicians then administer medicines to the sick? If it is time that is moulding everything, what need is there of medicines? ....If Time, according to thee, be the cause of acts, how can religious merit be acquired by persons performing religious acts?"[2]

A satisfactory answer to the question of freedom of will in the context of Indian thought is not that easy as it appears to be with reference to the above lines of the *Mahābhārata*. It is very complicated even as though, as we saw above, freedom of will is to be taken as a basic presupposition by any system of morality, because otherwise all talk about 'ought' and 'right' will be reduced simply to nonsense. We shall discuss these complications later. For the time being, let us concentrate on some more important presuppositions with which freedom of will is so intimately related that without a proper understanding of them it will not be possible to understand the question of freedom of will in the Indian context.

2. The Law of *Karma*

The most important presupposition of morality on which the entire Indian ethical system is based is called the law of *karma*. This law has its original source in the Vedic principle of *Ṛta*, which, amongst other things, envisages that an eternal moral order is involved in the very course of nature so that no action by anybody is lost in vain. He has to undergo the consequences of his action according to its merit or demerit. The law of *karma* which is a descendent of this basic moral principle is the law of the conservation of the results or consequences of an action. To be more specific, it has got two sides in its meaning, each one intimately related with the other: (1) No action is lost in vain *(kṛtapraṇāsaḥ);* one can in no case escape the consequences of his action, he is sure to reap whatever he has done. (2) No one is to bear the consequences of actions which he has not done himself (*akṛtābhyupagamaḥ*). That is, nobody is to reap the consequences of actions of other person. In the words of the *Mahābhārata*, the law stands thus: "In the world of men, no man reaps the consequences of another man's *karma*. Whatever one does, he is sure to reap the consequences thereof; for the consequences of the *karma* that is once done, can never be obviated."[3] If somebody does not exhaust the fruits of his actions in the present life, he has to assume a future life by way of rebirth, but he can in no way escape the consequences. Thus rebirth or *saṃsāra* is a necessary consequence of the law of *karma*.

It is this law of *karma* that gives morality a sound basis in the Indian context. Kant took God as a postulate of morality, because it is the belief in God which can guarantee virtue to be rewarded by happiness. Kant was a deontologist to the effect that he did not take conduciveness to any goal, such as happiness etc., to be the condition for any action to be moral but then he believed that virtue at some stage or other was sure to be rewarded by happiness. But what could be the guarantee for this reconciliation between virtue and happiness when we experience in several cases that virtuous suffer while those who commit vices rejoice? Only a belief in God could give such a guarantee. Because there is a (just) God behind the world, one should rest assured that such a reconciliation will be brought about sooner or later. For giving morality real significance thus, belief in God becomes necessary. In other words, belief in God according to Kant becomes a necessary postulate of morality. In the Indian context the same role is played by the law of *karma*. Every Indian system believes that virtuous acts produce good results, while acts of vice produce the evil ones. In other words, those who perform virtuous acts enjoy pleasure and happiness in this life or in a life beyond while those performing evil actions undergo pain and suffering.

But who or what guarantees this connection between good acts and happiness and between bad acts and suffering? God cannot be taken as forming the basis of this guarantee in the Indian context, because all the Indian systems of thought do not believe in God. But all of them believe in the reality and eternity of the law of *karma*, which is the standing principle of retribution. In the systems with no place for God, the principle works impersonally and independently, while in the systems with belief in God it works under his overall guidance. But even in the latter kind of systems it works in a sense independently because although God as a conscious being guides its working, He never interferes with its general principle of working. That is, in no case God exonerates the evil doer from the consequences of his evil doing nor does he ever let those suffer who have done virtuous acts. Hence, it is really the law of *karma* which guarantees virtue to be reconciled with happiness even in systems where there is a God. The law of *karma* is a basic postulate of the moral effort or practice in the Indian context.

3. Rebirth and *Saṃsāra*

The law of *karma* is seemingly very intimately related with the concept of rebirth or *saṃsāra*, so much so that the former cannot be conceived to be working significantly without the latter. Many a time we find that an evil doer enjoys happiness and a virtuous man suffers. The justification for this anomaly comes from the idea of a past life and future life. In having happiness here in this life the man might be undergoing the consequences of the good acts performed by him in the past life, while he waits for the painful consequences of his present misdeeds in a future life. Thus, along with the belief in the law of *karma*, belief in rebirth or *saṃsāra* may also be regarded as a postulate of moral life in India.

4. Immortality of the Soul

Rebirth presupposes the continuance of some element in man from one life to another which maintains his personal identity. This element is known as the soul or the *Ātman* in Indian thought. It is believed that this constitutes the essence of man and survives even after death. In other words, the soul is immortal. It is by virtue of this immortality that the soul survives the bodily death and migrates from one body to another to cause rebirth. Immortality of the soul is yet another postulate of morality in Indian ethics. It is on the presupposition of some element in man continuing from one life to another that the working of the law of *karma* with its retributive implications can be explained. And this continuing element is the immortal soul.

5. *Avidyā*

It seems to us that *avidyā* (ignorance) is the most basic presupposition of Indian ethics. This may sound paradoxical at the outset but as we enter into the matter, we find it as the basic postulate in the absence of which all talk about morality in the Indian context becomes meaningless. The whole gamut of the Indian thought in its philosophical, religious or ethical aspects hinges around the concepts of bondage and liberation. Hence, the essence of the moral efforts also lies in passing from the stage of bondage to that of liberation. Bondage is rebirth or *saṃsāra* and liberation is the cessation of rebirth. *Karma* which is at the base of rebirth is the real cause of bondage. But again *karma* is due to *rāga* (attachment) and *dveṣa* (aversion) towards the objects of the world and *rāga* and *dveṣa* in their final turn are the effects of *avidyā* or ignorance. So, ignorance is at the root of our *karmas* (actions)—right or wrong (*śubha* or *aśubha*). It is the general Indian view that *karmas*, right or worng, bind, because all of them are borne of ignorance in as much as they are the products of *vāsanās* which are generated within man due to *avidyā*. *Vāsanās* may be *śubha* (auspicious) or *aśubha* (inauspicious) which respectively lead to right or wrong actions. So, all moral distinctions between right and wrong are ultimately based on *avidyā*. In other words, distinctions have meaning only in a world of *avidyā* or ignorance. *Avidyā* is *anādi* (beginningless). So we are bound to take birth in ignorance. It should be life's singular aim to break the shackle of ignorance by our moral and religious effort. Morality by itself is not able enough to break the shackle completely, but it can pave the way for that. Thus *avidyā* is a moral postulate in the sense that without it in the background all talk about moral effort will lose significance. It is this which brings forth an occasion for man's moral effort. The counsels of personal morality such as *indriyanigraha, cittaśuddhi* etc. have meaning only in the background of passions and worldly attachments which are the results of *avidyā*. All counsels about social morality are meant ultimately for training the individuals for the path of individual morality and purity.

Moral effort has meaning not only in the background of *avidyā*, but also in the motivation for right and wrong actions. Good or bad desires prompt a person to perform good or bad actions. Desires or passions are the products of *avidyā*. An enlightened person will have no cause for work and if at all he works, he will perform only morally neutral *niṣkāma karmas*. As actions worth the name are basically the products of *avidyā*, it is the most basic postulate of morality in the Indian ethical setting.

It may be argued that taking *avidyā* and freedom both as postulates of morality in the same breath is self-contradictory. How can a man acting in ignorance be taken as working freely. Bondage and freedom are mutually opposite terms and cannot go together. This view may be apparently correct, until postulates of morality are seen in the right perspective and the concepts understood clearly.

Freedom is possible only after shaking off the shackles of ignorance or bondage. Indian philosophy says so. Real freedom in Indian view is possible only when one is liberated from ignorance. But the point needs to be understood that a life of bondage and a liberated life are two completely different ontological stages of being. The liberated man is said to be in a supraethical state. Freedom in the ethical context is freedom of the ignorant man. It is asked whether man in his present state (of bondage or ignorance) is in any sense free to act according to his own choice.

The question is not of freedom from the present state, but of freedom to choose and act in the present state. The answer is certainly 'yes' in the Indian context, otherwise a man in bondage will ever remain in that state. If he has no freedom to will or to act, how can he make efforts for salvation? We know that according to Indian view *avidyā* is *anādi* (beginningless), but it is not without end. It can be got rid of and that also by one's own personal effort. If there is no freedom to act, what will 'personal effort' mean? So, freedom to choose and act is there even in the state of bondage or ignorance. It is true that this ignorant being, a victim of delusion, acts sometimes blindly and mechanically, being prompted by the forces of *rāga* and *dveṣa*. It is equally true that breaking the shackle of ignorance is within our power. With all its light and grandeur the soul is all the time within us, only temporarily veiled by the curtain of ignorance. We are capable of seeing through the veils of ignorance. We have the capacity to make our choice for the better and free ourselves from the state of bondage. That we can remove ourselves the veil of ignorance by our own sincere efforts suggests by implication that we are free even in our state of ignorance to make efforts according to our choice. This is what ethical freedom means.

That ethical freedom is not jeopardised by ignorance can be argued in another way. It is *avidyā* which forms the basic reason for the working of the law of *karma*. The law of *karma* evinces that our present nature and dispostions are the results of our past *karmas* and our future will be built on our present *karmas* and whatever potencies are left of our past *karmas*. So, we are ever bound within a chain of determinism. Where is the freedom then? An answer to this question will obviously depend on our answer to the very frequently raised general question: Is there any scope for freedom under the law of *karma?* We will take up the issue for our detailed consideration in a succeeding chapter to argue that if the law of *karma* is properly understood, there is ample scope for freedom in it in the ethical sense of the term.

REFERENCES

1. *The Mahābhārata*, Vana Parva, 32, 3-20.
2. *Ibid.*, Śānti Parva, 139, 56-57.
3. *Ibid.*, Vana Parva, 213, 22-23.

CHAPTER VI

Development of Moral Beliefs and Ideas in Indian Thought

1. The Vedas

The history of Indian culture, philosophy or religion indisputably starts from what we call the Vedic age. As a matter of fact, morality too has its root in India in the Vedic age itself. By and large, the Vedas are regarded as treatises on various rituals directed towards various gods and goddesses. Ritualistic acts are prescribed as duties for men to perform. Whether these duties are moral or religious no clear distinction exists. Gods and goddesses are regarded as determining or controlling the overall destiny of man and therefore they must be pleased. Rituals associated with various sacrifices are taken as the most effective means to please the deities. Good is concieved mostly as the pleasure of gods and evil as their displeasure.

In tune with Hopkins it can be said a little differently that good is what the gods approve of and evil is what they disapprove of.[1] Though reference to sin has been made in various hymns, it has not been clearly defined anywhere. It seems, by and large, that sin has been concieved as a defilement clinging externally to somebody which can be expiated with external means. It is mostly deviation from the ritualistic details of a sacrifice and may be removed by pleasing a deity through rituals. Nevertheless, sin is sometimes understood in an ethical sense. For instance doing harm to friends, those who love, neighbours and strangers is sometimes understood as wrong. Similarly, lying is so often specified as great sin. But nowhere sin seems to have been conceived as an inner defilement. Any kind of sin can be expiated by observing prescribed ritualistic procedure. Sin is basically conceived an offence against the gods and goddesses. The idea of transference of sin from one to another is very common. If there is a concept of right and wrong, good and evil, virtue and vice, as there actually is (as is clear from the distinction between *Ṛju* and *Vṛjan*) in the Vedas, it is essentially externalistic in nature.

It is this externalistic and ritualistic concept of morality which developed to a great extent in the Dharmasūtras and Dharmaśāstras in its minutest details. But its intellectual side is hidden in these rituals. Sacrifice is the most powerful means for one to attain his ends, worldly or ultimate, and so every step in the sacrifice must be observed with greatest care. For this, knowledge of every step is essential. This emphasis on knowledge is often noted in sentences of the Brāhmṇas such as: 'He who has this knowledge conquers all directions,' 'He who has such knowledge becomes a light among his own people,' etc. In such sentences the Upaniṣadic emphasis upon knowledge for the attainment of the highest good is marked.

The above description of the Vedic morality should not lead us to conclude that an internal or finer concept of morality is completely absent from it. Furthermore, it has moral ideas and beliefs pertaining both to individual purity and social good. In a sense, the observance of the rituals themselves may be taken as a semblem of individual purity. Later on the Mīmāṃsakas have developed them with this sense in view. In the Dharmasūtras and Dharmaśāstras also, the elaborate observance of rituals, specially during the *gṛhasthāśrama*, has been prescribed as a means to individual purification.

We shall, however, like to draw here one's atttention to the concept of *Ṛta* as found in the *Ṛg Veda*. In a sense it is the fundamental source of the whole of Indian institution of moral life. Bloomfield remarks regarding *Ṛta* that "We have in connection with the *ṛta* a pretty complete system of ethics, a kind of counsel of Perfection."[2] '*Ṛta*', generally stands for order. The concept of *Ṛta* is very wide in its apeal in as much as it includes within it the ritual, the natural and the moral order all at the same time. But gradually it has come to be recognised as a repository of eternal moral order present in the very course of nature. However, its content is not very clear. After all, what concrete moral virtues it imbibes within it? By simply believing that there is an eternal moral order in the universe, it is not possible to spin a definite moral code around the principle of *Ṛta*.

In its later interpretations in the form of the law of *karma* it does not come about to be anything more than a principle of retribution, or more ethically speaking, a principle of justice. Moreover, it is not unambiguously evident whether it works purely independently or under the guidance or control of some god or goddess. Sometimes it seems that it rules supreme over even the world of gods and goddesses, but sometimes it seems to work under the guidance of gods like Varuṇa and Mitrā, especially the former, so often regarded as its custodian and charioteer. With this kind of characterisation of *Ṛta*, however, Truth as an important content of the principle comes to the fore. As Varuṇa is most prominently associated with Truth, so Truth may be taken to be the essential content of *Ṛta*, the most emphasized virtue in the Vedas and lying as the most emphasized sin or vice.

The story in the *Śatapatha Brāahmaṇa*[3] regarding the difference between the gods and the demons amply speaks of the important status that truth was given in the Vedas. The gods and the demons were both the descendents of Prajāpati and both inherited truth and falsehood of speech alike. The gods accepted later on truth and gave up falsehood, while the demons did just the reverse. A war between the gods and the demons brought victory to the former only because truth was on their side.

Besides truth, the virtues (or duties) which have been emphasized in the Vedas are *tapas, brahmacarya, śraddhā,* liberality (*dāna*), hospitality, friendship, non-cheating and non-violence. Similarly, the vices that have been so often emphasized are lying, gambling, arrogance etc. While some of these have social implications (liberality, hospitality, non-cheating etc.), others pertain to individual morality (*tapas, brahmacarya* etc.). Some of these, e.g., *dāna* and *tapas* have been much emphasized. These have found prominent place in the Upaniṣads also. *Dāna* mainly consists in offering gifts to priests and *tapas* means penance. It may either mean purposive endurance of physical sufferings or taking mental or physical strain for some specific purpose, specially perhaps for the purpose of expiating sin.

2. The Upaniṣads

As the Vedas are generally taken as treatises on ritualism, the Upaniṣads are regarded as treatises on *Jñāna* (knowledge). In the latter all such ideas as those of transmigration, *karma, saṃsāra, Mokṣa* etc. are, more or less, fully developed and it is felt that what is required for the attainment of *Mokṣa,* the highest end, is *Jñāna*, i.e. the knowledge of the evanscent character of the world. *Ajñāna* (ignorance) is the greatest vice which must be got rid of. The concept of sin is totally internalised here. What stains is not the outer action, but the root of the action i.e. the attachment to the world of senses. In other words, Sin, as Hopkins remarks, "is a question not of what one does, but of what one is."[4] But emphasis on *Jñāna* does not mean the negation of morality in the Upaniṣads. On the contrary, the role of morality has been emphasized as a pointer to the path of knowledge. One cannot embark on the path of knowledge without practising virtue. Both social and individual morality have found their due place, the latter gaining relatively more emphasis. In general, morality of being instead of morality of doing finds more prominent place in the Upaniṣads. How all this goes in the Upaniṣads, we can see in the following manner.

The Upaniṣads, on the whole, maintain that the ultimate reality underlying the universe is *Brahman* with whom the essential element in man, the *Ātman,* is identical (*tat tvam asi*). The ultimate end of man, *Mokṣa,* lies in knowing this identity of self with the *Brahman.* But this knowledge is not achieved by mere intellectual training. It requires purity of character and conduct. As *Kaṭha Up.* says, 'Not he who has not ceased from evil conduct (*duṣcarita*) can obtain Him by knowledge."[5] So good conduct is a necessary condition for realising the unity between the self and the *Brahman. Bṛhdāraṇyaka Up.* Clearly says that identity with *Brahman* is impossible for one who has not become "calm, subdued, quiet, enduring and collected."[6] These are virtues connected with individual morality. Similarly, in the *Taittirīya Up.* it is mentioned that when the student is about to depart from his teacher after getting education, the teacher exhorts the departing student by saying "Speak the truth (*satyam vada*), practise virtue (*dharmam cara*)."[7] This shows that the Upaniṣadic teacher is not only concerned about the intellectual training of the pupil, but about his moral perfectness also.

The ethical virtues (or duties) so often emphasized in the Upaniṣads are—*satya* (truth), *yajña* (sacrifice), *tapas* (penance) *dāna* (liberality), *adhyayana* (study of the Vedas), self-control, compassion, right dealing etc. One can see very clearly that the list includes virtues regarding both the individual and social morality. While *yajña, tapas, adhyayana,* self-control may be taken as examples of the former, truth, liberality, compassion, right dealing etc. may be taken as examples of the latter. However, there has been emphasis on the former virtues in the Upaniṣads than the latter. The pupil is instructed to observe *tapas, yajña, adhyayana* and *dāna* as part of *dharma.* In the *Praśna Up. tapas, brahmacarya* and *śraddhā* are regarded as indispensable conditions of knowledge. Similarly *sama* (tranquillity) and *dama* (self-control) are also duly emphasized.

While virtues like *yajña* (sacrifice), *tapas* (penance) and *dāna* (liberality) were given important place in the Vedas also, they acquire a more internalised import in the Upaniṣads. About *tapas* Dr. Surama Das Gupta remarks, "The concept of *tapas* in the Upaniṣads is, however, of a purer nature. It probably mans energy or self-effort, thought, self-control or study, and it is regarded not as a means to the attainment of mundane or extra-mundane benefits, but as a means to enlightenment or self-knowledge."[8] Thus, the crude and externalised concept of *tapas* in the Vedas is purified and internalised in the Upaniṣads. It is sometimes identified with *brahmacarya*, as in 1.15 of *Praśna Up. Yajña*, which was an elaborate process of ritual associated so often with animal sacrifices in the Vedas, is seen transformed in the Upaniṣads into what is called *upāsanā* or meditation. It is also taken in the sense of sacrifice, more especially in the sense of self-sacrifice, i.e., the sacrifice of egoistic desires. Here *Yajña* takes a more purified form, having set a higher aim to attain self-knowledge rather than gaining control over mere worldly pleasure through the ritual of animal sacrifices in the Vedas. Similarly, *dāna* also gets a wider connotation. In the Vedas it was mostly associated with gifts to the priests, but here in the Upaniṣads it becomes an ideal of charity that must govern all social relations. It implies general attitude of helpfulness towards others even at one's own cost. Most emphasis is laid on the ideal of *dāna* in the Upaniṣads. It is said that one must not lose an opportunity of making gifts under any circumstances,[9] and that one should give (gifts) with *śraddhā*, with modesty, with sympathy and with fear. Finer social virtues are associated with *dāna*.

The Upaniṣads mainly emphasize on knowledge as the means to final liberation. Yet, the importance of ethical virtues of conduct and character—both social and individual—is never ignored. These moral virtues are not valuable in themselves, but they are important as a means for purifying the spirit by improving one's character, so that he becomes fit for attaining knowledge or enlightenment.

3. The Smṛtis

Surama Das Gupta characterises the ethics of the Smṛtis as follows: "From the Brāhmaṇas onwards, through the Sūtras literature down to the Smṛtis, we find that the tendency towards the external observance of rituals has been joined up with the notion of social good as well. A definite scheme of life of a man with detailed instructions for his duties in every stage of life has been chalked out. This scheme tries to reconcile the supremacy of Vedic injunctions, and the necessity of social virtues on the one hand, and the virtues for self-purification for the final enlightenment on the other. It seems that it tries to harmonise these two types of standards mentioned above which, being of opposite nature, should have otherwise drifted apart."[10]

Smṛti literature is generally taken to include the Dharmasūtras, the Dharmaśāstras, the Purāṇas and the two epics. I am taking the nomenclature here only for the former two and feel that the above characterisation of Surama Dasgupta in respect of them is very apt. To a great extent it is apt for the epics also, but that I will take up later on. The Dharmasūtras and the Dharmaśāstras on the one side seem to revive the Vedic ritualism in its most elaborate form once again and that way they seem to mark a degeneration in Indian thought in the light of the height of philosophical thought as achieved in the Upaniṣads. Sin is conceived in the fashion of the Vedas quite externally. Transferrence of sins to others is a common conception and expiation can be effected through purely external means. This is why John Mckenzie remarks about the conception of sin in the Dharmaśāstras: "It is something that is as separable from the individual as the coat he wears."[11]

But, on the other hand, the Smṛtis present a very elaborate code of human conduct in all its varied relationships and in all the various stages of its development. In this scheme all the virtues and duties related to social as well as idividual life are mentioned. The whole thing is done under a threefold scheme of *dharmas—sādhāraṇa dharma, varṇa dharma* and *āśrama dharma*. Right from the age of the Vedas, the Indian society is divided into four classes, with specific duties assigned to each class. That the *āśrama dharma* could not be clearly developed in the Vedas is indicated in enough measure. It is in the Upaniṣads that the *āśrama dharma* is fully developed with its specifications. As is well-known, it pertains to the fourfold scheme of individual life. The Smṛtis give an elaborate description of the *varṇa* and *āśrama dharmas*, specifying duties of each individual in accordance with his *varṇa* and *āśrama*. Rituals connected specially with the *āśrama dharma* are also elaborately mentioned. It is the duty of everyone to observe them strictly in accordance with the *āśrama* of life he belongs to. The *sādhāraṇa dharmas* are the *dharmas* (virtues and duties) to be followed by everyone irrespective of his *varṇa* or *āśrama*. They are common duties to be observed by all.

These duties contain in themselves duties (or virtues) relating to social morality as well as those pertaining to individual purity. For example, let us take Manu's ten *dharmas—dhṛti* (patience), *kṣamā* (forgiveness), *dama* (self-control), *asteya* (non-stealing), *śauca* (cleanliness), *indriyanigraha* (control of the senses) *dhi* (intellect or wisdom), *vidyā* (learning), *satya* (truthfulness) and *akrodha* (absence of anger). Whereas *kṣamā, asteya, truthfulness* etc. are social virtues, the rest are those that promote individual morality, specifically meant for individual purity. Besides these *akārpaṇya*, hospitality and non-violence are also so often emphasized by Manu. More exhaustive lists with social and individual implications may be cited from Āpastamba, Gautama etc. also.

In the Smṛtis we may find elements of both external and internal, social and individual concepts of morality. With emphasis laid on the observance of various sacraments and rituals, one may conclude that their purely externalistic nature lays emphasis only on ritualistic and ceremonial actions. But that is not wholly true. Side by side with the external acts, internal virtues have also been emphasized and their more important role in morality is also recognised. For example, Gautama, after laying down a list of forty sacraments which are to be observed by a good man, immediately proceeds to lay down what he calls the "eight good qualities of the soul" and remarks, "He who is sanctified by these forty sacraments, but whose soul is destitute of eight good qualities will not be united with *Brahman*, nor does he reach his heaven. But he, who is sanctified by a few only of these forty sacraments, and whose soul is endowed with the eight excellent qualities, will be united with *Brahman*, and will dwell in heaven."[12]

This is a clear indication of the sense of distinction between external and internal concepts of morlaity of which the latter is given greater value. The eight good qualities of the soul are enumerated as follows—compassion for all creatures, forbearance, freedom from zealousy, purity, quietism, auspiciousness, freedom from avarice and freedom from covetousness. Even Mckenzie, a very unsympathetic critic of ancient Hindu ethics, recognises the above fact as revealed from his statement, "The emphasis has been on overt acts and not on the motive from which they have sprung. Sin has been regarded as an evil substance that clings to one bringing defilement, and its removal may be effected through physical means. But it is right that we should give attention to some signs of a deeper and more spiritual view of morality which are to be found here and there . . . . there are a few passages which stand out markedly as revealing the fact that even where the human mind is most steeped in ritualism there may be present a truly ethical sense which will sometimes express itself. Gautama, for example, deals much in the orthodox way with the *saṃskāras* or sacraments, but. . . . he recognises that the inner ethical virtue of the soul stand on a different and higher place. . ."[14] Similarly, if we go through Āpastamba's list of virtues and vices, (1.9.23. 5-6) we shall mark the same note of the internal concept of morality. In a similar vein the Vaśiṣṭha sūtra mentions: "Neither austerities, not (the study of) the Veda, nor (the performance of) the *agnihotra*, nor lavish liberality can ever save him whose conduct is vile and who has stayed from his path of duty. The Vedas do not purify him who is deficient in good conduct, though he may have learnt them altogether with the six Aṅgas. . . . As the beauty of a wife causes no joy to a blind man, even so all the four Vedas together with the six Aṅgas and sacrifices give no happiness to him who is deficient in good conduct."[15]

Similarly, the emphasis in Vedas on the attainment of earthly pleasure and heaven through observance of prescribed rituals and ceremonies can also be seen in the Dharmasūtras and Dharmaśāstras, together with the idea of the *summum bonum* as *Mokṣa* or as the identity of soul with the *Brahman*, as found in the Upaniṣads. Both elements of social and individual morality are very well present in them except that virtues relating to individual purity are seemingly more prominent.

4. The Epics (Specially the *Mahābhārata* including the *Bhagavadgītā*)

The *Rāmāyaṇa* and the *Mahābhārata* are the two great epics of the Indian tradition. They are very popular among the Hindu masses as the repository of great ethical and human values. Presented in the form of stroies, both speak of the ultimate defeat of the evil forces by the good. In their essential force and implication they are out and out moral. The *Rāmāyaṇa* inculcates within its body almost all the moral ideals which may be connected with the human life in all its personal, domestic, social and political aspects in their fullest perfection. Ethical precepts and ideals are not talked of separately, they are intertwined within the flow of the story itself in all its steps. Only a wise man has to derive his lesson from there.

The *Mahābhārata*, however, deals with the moral precepts separately also, especially in the form of moral counsels from Bhīṣma, Yudhiṣṭhira, and others. The *Bhagavadgītā*, which forms a part of the *Mahābhārata*, may be treated as a treatise on ethics itself. The ethical ideals presented in the *Bhagavadgītā* very adequately speak of the evolutionary character of Indian moral thought. They show how Indian moral thought has developed from its crude and rudimentary form in the Vedas to a very fine and elevated position as given in the *Bhagavadgītā*. We shall deal here with the general moral atmosphere of the *Mahābhārata* with special reference to the *Bhagavadgītā* in somewhat a detailed form to mark the nature and extent of this evolution.

The *Mahābhārata*, by and large, may be taken as giving vent to the high ideals of social morality, although the importance of Vedic ritualism and the virtues of individual purity have not been totally ignored. It is not only that the *Mahābhārata* takes the social good or the social welfare as the primary aim of moral conduct, rather in its sources also morality, according to it, is rooted to a great extent in the social customs and traditions as well as in the consensus of the people of the society. Dr. Surama Das Gupta seems to be correct when she says, "The standards of morality as preached in the *Mahābhārata* .... recognise both the absolute and relative nature of morality. There the ideals of social progress through the maintenance of social equilibrium are partly determined by scriptures and partly by the standard of public good, the latter sometimes superseding the injunction of the scriptures and sometimes being supplementary to them."[16]

Both the *Mahābhārata* and the *Gītā* seem to hold with the Indian tradition that the social and individual order are to be best maintained by observing the *Varṇāśrama dharma*. But along with these they advise following certain general duties such as: *ahiṃsā, satya, akrodha, priyavacana, dayā, prema, svārthatyāga, paranindātyāga* (non-injury, truth, avoidance of anger, speaking sweet language, compassion and love for all creatures, avoidance of egoism, avoidance of speaking ill of others) etc. The ideals of social good such as *lokasthiti* (maintenance of social order), *lokasiddhi* (preservation of social customs etc.) *lokasaṃgraha* (social equilibrium) *lokakalyāṇa* (welfare of the society) and *lokayātrā* (social progress) are so often mentioned and emphasized.

But the ideal of final liberation, *Mokṣa*, has not been neglected. The *Mahābhārata* counsels that those who aim at attaining the final good should practise the ordinary virtues as mentioned above, but they must pass beyond them through yoga. For that self-purification is necessary and virtues like self-control, equanimity, quietitude, forbearance, indifference to pleasure and pain are emphasized. Truthfulness as a virtue is, however, emphasized althrough.

One special feature of the ethics of the *Mahābhārata* and the *Gītā* is that they propound an out and out internal conception of morality. Of course, the authority of the Vedic injunctions and ritualism is not completely ruled out, but it is emphasized that what rewards or stains is not the outer action but the inner motive, will or intention. So, while doing actions, Vedic or non-Vedic, narrow egoistic passions should be avoided. One should do his duty selflessly.

The aim of our actions should be either social good or individual liberation. Even performance of Vedic rituals with narrow egoistic aims is discouraged and depreciated. Lord Krishna speaks with contempt of those who simply hold fast to the words of the Veda, but whose souls are stained with lust and whose only aim is to attain pleasure in the heaven.[17] So what is required for morality is inner purity. Mere external work will not do. Little sin is committed by him who does work without knowing its bad result. What stains is bad motive and ill will, not the action.

This actually leads to the ideal of *niṣkāma karma*, the essence of the ethics of the *Bhagavadgītā*. If one is asked to describe the ethics of the *Bhagavadgītā* in the shortest possible way, it will be, to our mind, simply in terms of the advice to practise *niṣkāma karma* and *svadharma*. In other words, the ethics of the *Gītā* is the ethics of *niṣkāma karma* and *svadharma*. The former means passionless actions and the latter means one's duty in accordance with one's station in life as determined by one's *varṇa* and *āśrama*. Actions without attachment do not bind. One has to free his mind of egoistic passions. If the heart is pure and all actions are done without any lust for result, that is the greatest sign of morality according to the *Gītā*. One has to follow one's own *dharma*, i.e., duties prescribed for one's own *varṇa* and *āśrama*. That also is the greatest moral duty. The ethical virtues on which *Gītā* emphasized are very exhaustively mentioned in Chapter XVI.2-3 as follows—non-violence, truthfulness, absence of anger, absence of jealousy, absence of greed, absence of enmity and egoism, charity to all beings, tranquillity, tenderness, steadiness, persistence, forgiveness, patience and modesty. However, some of the Vedic duties such as sacrifice, gift and austerity are also emphasized sometimes.

It is clearly said in Chapter XVIII.5 that "acts of sacrifice, gift and austerity ought not to be abandoned, rather they should be performed; for sacrifice, gift and austerity are purifiers of the wise." Similarly, importance of *tapas, yajña* and *dāna* has been emphasized in the context of fairly broad and improved meanings given to them. The word '*tapas*' has not been used here in the sense of inflicting any kind of pain or torture upon oneself, it has rather been used in the broad sense of cultivating restraint of body, mind and speech. It has been delienated that only genuine *tapas* is performed with a pure and elevated aim. *Tapas* performed with a sense of arrogance for name and fame or a *tapas* performed for the destruction of the enemy is no real *tapas*. *Gītā* therefore distinguishes between three kinds of *tapas:* (1) that which is undertaken with a view to torturing oneself or others, known as the *tāmasika tapas;* (2) that which is undertaken with a sense of arrogance for personal name and fame, known as *rājasika tapas;* and (3) that which is undertaken with a sense of faith (*śraddhā*) and disinterestedness, known as the *sāttvika tapas.*[18] The first one is of the lowest type, the second one is of the higher type and the third one is of the highest type. From another standpoint, *Gītā* again distinguishes between three kinds of *tapas*—those related to body, those related to speech and those related to mind. Showing respect to gods, teachers, Brahmins and wise people, purity of body, continence and non-violence are instances of bodily *tapas*. Truthful but harmless, pleasant and beneficial speech, and study of the scriptures are examples of *tapas* related to speech. Silence, mental equilibrium, tranquillity, self-control and simplicity are *tapas* related to the mind.[19] Similarly, *Yajña* and *dāna* also have been understood rather broadly and have been characterised as *sāttvika*, *rājasika* and *tāmasika*. A *Yajña* performed with cool mind according to the procedure laid down in the scriptures and purely with a sense of duty without any desire for personal gain is *sāttvika yajña*. A *Yajña* which is carried out only to show one's wealth with a sense of pride and arrogance is *rājasika yajña* and a *Yajña* performed without faith, without following the scriptural procedure and without *dāna* etc. is *tāmasika yajña*.[20] *Dāna* which is given to proper persons at proper place and time and without any sense of personal benefit is *sāttvika dāna*. A *dāna* which is made out of hope for future benefits with an unwilling heart is *rājasika dāna* and a *dāna* made to improper persons at improper places with disrespect and negligence is *tāmasika dāna*.[21]

5. The Systems

Indian philosophical thoughts in its embryonic form were laid down in the Vedas and more particularly in the Upaniṣads. Later on, these stray philosophical thoughts gave rise to organised philosophical systems. There are altogether nine recognised systems in the ancient Indian philosophical tradition, six of which are known as orthodox systems due to their supposed loyalty to Vedas, and the rest three as unorthodox or heterodox systems because of their disloyality to the Vedas. The Nyāya, the Vaiśeṣika, the Sāṃkhya, the Yoga, the Pūrva Mīmāṃsā (or simply Mīmāṃsā) and the Uttar Mīmāṃsā (or the Vedānta) come under the former group, and the Cārvāka, the Buddhism and the Jainism come under the second group. This grouping, however, does not imply that systems under any particular group keep exactly similar viewpoints on general philosophical or ethical questions. They rather differ importantly among themselves. In some very essential points Buddhism and Jainism have similarities with the so-called orthodox systems, while all of them sharply differ from the Cārvāka system.

So far as the question of loyality to the Vedas is concerned, only Pūrva Mīmāṃsā has an unqualified loyality to the Vedas. But the Vedas believe in various gods and goddesses, while the Mīmāṃsā does not believe in any god at all. In a general sense, however, not only the so-called orthodox systems, but Buddhism and Jainism too may be regarded as indebted to the Vedas and the upaniṣads in their general philosophical or ethical approach. There is one important agreement, however, amongst the so-called heterodox systems and that is regarding the strong oppositions of each to the Vedic ritualism and the duties of individuals based on their *varṇa*. But so far as their loyality to a spiritualistic and humanistic ethics and religion is concerned, Buddhism and Jainism both have essential agreement with most of the systems which come under the so-called orthodox school. All these points will be clear when we will take up below a very brief and general survey of the ethical beliefs and ideas of the individual systems.

Every philosophical system has certain necessary ethical consequences, which may be deduced out of it. Unfortunately, such derivations have not been made in case of Indian philosophical systems. However, this does not amount to saying that such derivations cannot be made. Instead, we shall deal here with the ethical norms and values which each system by itself has incorporated within it. No system is completely devoid of such values. It is possible that these values may not be the direct logical consequences of the metaphysical presuppopsitions of a particular system, but they do not go against the broad tenor of the system. In other words, they do not look like being imposed on it from outside; they have a compatibility with the general environment of the system. The systems again differ in the details of the ethical values they preach, but in their essential spirit almost all of them (with the solitary exception of the Cārvāka) agree. They also agree in their basic ethical presuppositions, such as belief in *karma*, *saṃsāra*, *avidyā*, *Mokṣa* etc. Again, all of them have both elements of social (or objective) and individual (or subjective) morality in as much as all of them preach important social virtues and duties and also norms and practices leading to individual *cittaśuddhi* and spiritual development.

It has generally been alleged against the Indian systems, and as a matter of fact against the whole of Indian tradition, that moral life has not been given an ultimate significance. The end of life is *Mokṣa* which is attainable through *Jñāna* (knowledge). Bondage, the opposite of *Mokṣa*, is due to ignorance (*ajñāna*), and it is only *Jñāna* which can remove *ajñāna*. Morality which mainly consists in the performance of right actions actually binds people. Actions, right or wrong, all have a binding effect, because all of them produce results or effects which, according to the law of *karma*, one is bound to undergo. So, *karma* is actually the cause of rebirth and *saṃsāra*. Right actions produce good results in as much as they can give prosperity and pleasure in this life and an elevated and happy life after rebirth too. But rebirth of any nature is bondage after all.

Actions (and hence morality) in a way are all to be forsaken in the ultimate analysis so that one can be finally free from the shackles of bondage and rebirth.

The allegation cannot be rejected outright. What has been said in the preceding paragraph is the general Indian approach towards actions. But one must guard against two misconceptions that may crop up in one's mind (and they have hovered over many Western minds). The misconceptions are: (1) morality, specially social morality, has been given a subsidiary place in human life or, in other words, the role of morality comes in life only as a matter of passing reference; and (2) for a man who has crossed the level of ordinary morality on his way to *jñāna* has absolutely no concern with morality. These are misconceptions *par excellence* with which many Western thinkers have been haunted. It is really on the strength of these that they have so often tried to highlight a basically non-ethical character of Indian philosophical tradition. It is a fact that morality has been given only a preparatory value in the ultimate Indian scheme of life, but so far as it goes it has been taken seriously as a very important aspect of life. Only Sāṃkhya and Vedānta seem to preach on the apparent level that *Jñāna* can be attaind directly by means of meditation etc. and for that the pursuit of a moral life is not necessarily required. But we will see that they also do not, as a matter of fact, ignore the role and significance of morality in life. Other systems such as the Nyāya-Vaiśeṣika, the Yoga, the Mīmāṃsā the Rāmānuja Vedānta and the two non-orthodox systems—Buddhism and Jainism—very explicitly emphasize the inevitable role of morality in taking one to the path of *Jñāna* which is virtually liberation. What is prohibited are actions done with egoistic passion and desire. It is such actions which bind. Non-attached actions have never been prohibited. They have rather always been encouraged.

(a) ***The Nyāya-Vaiśeṣika***

The Nyāya-Vaiśeṣika clearly maintains that the actions prompted by the three *doṣas*—*icchā, dveṣa,* and *moha*—bind. Therefore, they must be got rid of. This means what is required for that necessarily includes a path of morality consisting of the *sādhāraṇa* and the *varṇāśrama dharmas.* The *sādhārana dharmas* include obviously ethical virtues and duties. They are: *śraddhā* for *dharma,* harmlessness, benevolence, truthfulness, freedom from desire for undue possession, freedom from lust, purity of intention, absence of anger, bathing, absence of use of purifying substances, devotion to deities, fasting, and non-neglect of duties.[22] The

Varaṇāśrama dharmas include duties for a Brahmana, Kṣatriya, Vaiśya and Śūdra as well as duties in accordance with one's station in life, such as, *Brahmacarya, Gṛhastha, Vānaprastha* and *Sannyāsa.* Similarly, there are actions called *adharmas* which are prohibited. They are: (1) Those actions which are prohibited by the Śāstras and contrary to *dharma,* such as, harmfulness, falsehood, undue possession etc., (2) Non-performance of actions enjoined in the scriptures, (3) Neglect of duties.

(b) *The Sāṃkhya-Yoga*

Similarly, Sāṃkhya does not discourage virtuous conduct. It only envisages that good acts should be done in a spirit of complete detachment. Sāṃkhya also depreciates the Vedic rituals, specially those which incur *hiṃsā.* But Sāṃkhya believes in the distinction of good and bad deeds, the former brings one nearer to liberation and the latter throws him farther from it. In accordance with its metaphysical belief of the reality of three *guṇas,* it believes in ethically significant three kinds of actions: (1) *sāttvika* actions which consist in kindness, restraint of sense-organs, freedom from hatred etc. (2) *rājasika* actions which consist in passion, anger, greed, violence, discontent, faultfinding, rudeness etc. (3) *tāmasika* actions which consist in madness, intoxication, lassitude, drowsiness, lust worthlessness, impurity etc. Of these, the first kind of actions leads one towards the attainment of liberation. They are good actions which must be followed. Again, the eightfold discipline which the yoga system prescribes for the attainment of liberation consists among other steps also of *yama* and *niyama* which are as much necessary parts of the discipline as other steps are and which are out and out ethical in significance. The former, by the large, relates to social morality and the latter to individual morality. *Ahiṃsā, satya, asteya, brahmacarya,* and *aparigraha* come under the former and *śauca* (cleanliness) *saṃtoṣa* (contentment), *tapas* (austerity and forbearance), *svādhyāya* (study) and making God the motive of all actions (Īśvara-prāṇidhāna) come under the latter. Thus we can see that both the elemetns of social and individual morality form necessary part of the discipline leading to *Mokṣa.* How can it be said, then, that morality has got only a negligible place in the scheme of life as envisaged by the Indian systems of thought?

(c) *The Mīmāṃsā*

In Mīmāṃṣā morality or *dharma* gets the highest place. It is directly through the observance of *dharma* that *Mokṣa* is attained. *Dharma,* however, as understood in Mīmāṃsā is different from ordinary morality. It is the observance of whatever is enjoined in the Vedas with unquestioning loyality and the Vedic injunctions refer here to the ritualistic texts. Thus *dharma* consists mainly in the performance of sacrificial actions as enjoined in the Vedas and the non-performance of the prohibited actions. As a matter of fact, the Mīmāṃsakas speak of the three kinds of actions: (1) *Kāmya karmas,* i.e. actions done with a particular motive or end in view, (2) *pratisiddha karmas,* i.e. forbidden actions, and (3) *nityanaimittika karmas,* i.e. unconditional duties to be done either daily or on certian specific ceremonial occasions. The former two kinds of actions bind, but the performance of the third one removes the *saṃskāras* of the past actions and leads to *Mokṣa.* The observance of this form of *karmas* needs control of passions. They are to be performed with a complete and exclusive sense of duty. They require a sense of complete disinterestedness. Thus in the form of *nityanaimittika karmas* the Mīmāṃsakas preach categorically imperative actions like those of Kant.

(d) *The Śaṃkara Vedānta*

Śaṃkara Vedānta is the system which again does not seem to give morality enough importance in the scheme of life oriented towards liberation. According to Śaṃkara, *Mokṣa* is *Jñāna,* in the attainment of which morality has not to play any necessary or indispensable role. However, the observance of morality is beneficial in as much as it helps the soul being free from the impurity of the senses and various egoistic passions and desires. That in its turn makes the path to *Jñāna* easier and smoother. The duties which Śaṃkara seems to prescribe in this connection are for the most part duties related with the *varṇāśrama dharma.* Besides these, Śaṃkara also prescribes such duties as Vedic study, sacrifice, alms giving, penance and fasting. But these he takes as remote means to knowledge. Amongst the more approximate or closer ones he counts virtues related with individual discipline such as tranquillity, self-restraint, renunciation, patience and concentration.[23]

However, one thing must be realised that although Śaṃkara has not given any basic importance to a moral life due to his predominantly *Jñāna*-oriented system, it is not correct to say that there is no scope within this system for morality, especially for social morality. This apprehension is mainly due to the identity that Śaṃkara preaches between the individual self and *Brahman* and also due to his treating the world as *māyā.* The former is alleged to remove all real distinctions between good and evil, which is the foundation stone of morality and the latter does not leave any scope for a significant and real worldly social life. Both these apprehensions are based on misconception and misunderstanding. Dr. Radhakrishnan has taken great pains to show in his *Eastern Religions and Western Thought* and other works that Śaṃkara's theory of individual self and world leaves ample scope for morality in man's life. Śaṃkara's theory of the identity between self and *Brahman*, instead of robbing morality of its real significance, really gives it a sound metaphysical foundation. The virtues of universal brotherhood, love, compassion etc. which are the keynotes of social morality find their real meaning only when it is understood that all people, in fact all the sentient creatures, are basically one; the distinctions are only external and artificial. Śaṃkara does not regard this world as totally illusory to make social life impossible. From the practical standpoint the world is fully real; only it has not the ultimate reality. Moreover, the identity between self and *Brahman* does not mean that the distinction between good and evil has no real meaning.

It is to be kept in mind that according to Śaṃkara the identity between the self and the *Brahman* is the essential nature of the reality. In its present worldly or bodily state the self is alienated from *Brahman* and is in a state of ignorance, illusion or bondage. In this state it is liable to all kinds of evils and hence the distinction between good and evil is to be made. As Dr. Radhakrishnan remarks, " 'I am *Brahman*' does not mean direct identity of the active self with the ultimate *Brahman* but only the identity of the real self when the false imposition is removed. The ethical problems arise, because there is the constant struggle between the infinite character of the soul and the finite dress in which it has clothed itself."[24]

(e) ***The Rāmānuja Vedānta***

In the Viśiṣṭādvaita system of Rāmānuja, ethics seems to play a very dominant role inasmuch as it contributes directly and significantly towards the attainment of *Mokṣa* and all the important ethical virtues follow directly from the very nature of God. God, according to Rāmānuja, possesses not only the metaphysical qualities of all-powerfulness etc., but also the highly esteemed moral qualities, such as, forgiveness, compassion, straightforwardness, gentleness, tenderness etc....God directs all these auspicious qualities towards the dispelling of darkness and evil from the path of his creatures. For example forgiveness in God is for the guilty who has since repented and seen the error of his ways. Compassion in God is for the suffering creatures. Gentleness is for the shy and the timid.[25] Taking lesson from God's possession of the moral qualities and their use in the above manner, man also should inculcate and cultivate these moral qualities for the benefit of the ignorant, the poor, the weak etc. The greatest moral virtue of man is to imitate God's moral qualities in his practice and behaviour. According to Rāmānuja, *Mokṣa* is ultimately achieved by the grace of God, but for winning this grace, it is necessary that man imitates the moral qualities of God and lives a strictly moral life. To imitate God is the greatest devotion to Him.

Even by analysing the steps of what Rāmānuja calls the *upāsanā* or *bhakti* of God, we can see that, in the main, only elements of individual and social morality are present therein. *Upāsanā* is constituted by abstention (*viveka*), freeness of mind (*vimoha*), repetition (*abhyāsa*), works (*kriyā*), virtuous conduct, freedom from dejection (*anāvaṣāda*) and absence of exultation (*anuddharṣa*).[26] The steps are also clearly defined as follows: Abstention means keeping the body clean from impure food, impure either due to species (such as flesh of certain animals) or abode of accidental cause (such as food into which a hair or the like has fallen). Freeness of mind means absence of attachment to desires. By works is understood the performance, according to one's ability, of the five great sacrifices. By virtuous conduct is meant the cultivation of virtues like truthfulness, honesty, kindness, liberality, gentleness and absence of covetousness. Freedom from dejection means highness of spirit and cheerfulness. Absence of exultation means absence of overgreat satisfaction.

Analysis of the various elements in the act of *upāsanā* brings out the involvment of both personal and social morality in it. Besides these, Rāmānuja also allows an important place to the *varṇāśrama dharmas* in the scheme of moral life. The observance of these *dharmas* eradicates the fruits of the past *karmas* and thus paves the way for liberation.[27] Rāmānuja also emphasizes the need and value of the *niṣkāma karmas*. Endorsing with full heart the *Gītā* ideal of the *niṣkāma karmas*, Rāmānuja seems preferring *Karma-yoga* to *Jñāna-yoga* in the attainment of *Mokṣa*.[28]

(f) *Buddhism and Jainism*

We have drawn above an outline of the ethical beliefs and ideas of the six so-called orthodox systems. Let us now come to the so-called unorthodox systems like Buddhism, Jainism and the Cārvāka. As we have already said, Buddhism and Jainism under the same unorthodox group share between themselves many essential ethical beliefs and ideas of the orthodox systems, which may also be called the Hindu system. For example, the basic ethical presuppositions of these two schools are the same as those of the Hindu system, viz., *karma, saṃsāra, ajñāna, Mokṣa* etc. Both these systems preach the objective and subjective moralities, with emphasis upon the latter, as in the Hindu system. The points in which they importantly differ from Hinduism are: (1) their firm rejection of the Vedic ritualism and (2) their rejection of the classification of duties based on *varṇavyavasthā*. Let us see some of the specific points regarding Buddhism and Jainism separately.

As we have said above, Buddhism in many respects is very near to Hinduism. In ethical teachings of the two religions also there is an essential similarity. The difference mainly lies in (1) the rejection by Buddhism of the ritualistic and ceremonial aspects that were very strongly prevalent in Hinduism under the influence of the Vedas and (2) making the concept of *karma* more ethical. Mckenzie seems to be right when he remarks, "Buddhism developed directly out of Brahmanism, retaining much of what was most characteristic in the Brahmanical point of view. Indeed, there is a sense in which it may be said that Buddhism in its original form was really a reformulation on ethical line of what was most fundamental in the existing systems of thought. The ritualistic and magical elements were rejected or relegated to a less determinative position, and the strictly ethical consequences of certain ideas which had become firmly established in Hindu mind, especially *karma* and *saṃsāra*, were brought out."[29] In the Hindu systems actions considered to be helpful towards the attainment of *Mokṣa*, are mainly ritualistic ones as enjoined in the Vedas or actions in accordance with the *varṇāśrama vyavasthā*. But in Buddhism such actions are of the nature of both social and individual morality. Mckenzie rightly says, "In the teaching of the Buddha... *karma* was largely ethicised. The only acts which were regarded as meritorious were moral acts and belief in the efficacy of rites and ceremonies was condemned as heresy."[30] For example, by rejecting the efficacy and value of Vedic sacrificialism, Buddhism becomes able to emphasize *ahiṃsā* as a real moral virtue in its truest and purest spirit. *Ahiṃsā* was given a positive meaning also and that meaning was love. Thus, the virtue of love was given a prominent place in the ethical teaching of Buddhism. In general, we can say that as virtues (or duties) of social morality Buddhism emphasizes the following: humility, charity, love, gratefulness, sympathy, forgiveness, veracity, justice etc. And again as virtues of individual morality, it emphasizes the following: self-restraint, temperance, contentment, gentleness, celibacy, patience, purity etc.[31]

However, the above is only a general account of the Buddhist virtues of individual and social morality. Speaking somewhat specifically, we may see that the characteristic Buddhist ethical discipline is contained in the eightfold path that Buddha himself gives out as leading to the highest end *Nirvāṇa*. This eightfold path consists of right view, right thought, right speech, right action, right living, right effort, right mindfulness and right concentration. Of these, the first two come under what is known as *prajñā*, the next three come under *śīla* and the last three under *samādhi*. More specifically speaking, it is *śīla* which represents Buddhist morality. Let us see the items under *śīla*.

The first is right speech. This consists in refraining from telling a lie, back-biting, harsh talk and idle gossip. Moreover, according to it our speech should be free from any kind of ill will and selfish interest. The second is right action, which consists in the observance of five precepts known as *Pañcaśīla*. These are: (1) Not to kill, but to practise harmlessness and compassion (*ahiṃsā*), (2) Not to take that which is not given, but to practise charity and generosity (*asteya*), (3) Not to commit sexual misconduct, but to practise chastity and self-control (*brahmacarya*), (4) Not to indulge in false speech, but to practise sincerity and honesty (*satya*), (5) Not to take intoxicating drinks or drugs, but to practise restraint and mindfulness. The third, i.e. right living, consists in adopting a just, honestly earned and undeceitful means of livelihood which does not debar others of their just rights of the same.

Of the three *śīlas* mentioned above, the most imporant is obviously the *pañcaśīla* coming under right action. This is essential according to Buddhism for all, for the laity and the saint or mendicant alike. But Buddhism also speaks of *aṭṭhaśīla* and *dasaśīla*, the former meant for persons in the laity who are comparatively less attached to family life and the latter meant for monks. The *aṭṭhaśīla* includes the following three, besides the above five: abstaining from taking untimely meals: abstaining from dancing, singing, music etc. and from using garlands, pefumes, cosmetics, and personal adorements; abstaining from using high seats. The *dasaśīla* includes the following two besides the *aṭṭhaśīla*: sleeping on a mat spread on the ground (It is really not different from the eighth one of the *aṭṭhaśīla*, because it is virtually a consequence of that) and abstaining from the use of gold and silver.

We can see that most of the virtues included under *aṭṭha-* or *dasaśīla* are virtues of austerity and penance very closely related tot he Upaniṣadic conception of *tapas*. They are specifically meant for withdrawing the mind from the attractions of the world, so that it could be directed towards the attainment of the spiritual goal, *Nirvāṇa*. To a large extent virtues relating to individual purity have been exphasized in Buddhism also, although amongst the virtues to be inculcated by the laity, those relating to social morality have been emphasized. These virtues have been given a greater and purer ethical meaning than they were given in the Hindu systems.

Like Buddhism, Jainism also is very near to Hinduism in matters of essential ethical teachings. But it is nearer to Buddhism that to Hinduism in one important respect of rejecting Vedic ceremonialism and sacrificialism. Like Buddhism, Jainism also takes *ahiṃsā* to be the most important ethical virtue and consequently denounces the Vedic sacrifices. In the observance of *ahiṃsā*, Jainism rather surpasses even Buddhism. But in so doing it sometimes invites annoyance and even ridicule. In the observance of ascetic virtues also, Jainism goes farther than Buddhism, especially in the case of the monks and in this it seems more influenced by the Hindu concept of *tapas*. In general, however, the Jaina morality consists in the essential observance of the *pañcamahāvratas*, which are the ingredients of right conduct. For the attainment of *Mokṣa*, Jainism prescribes a threefold path known as *triratna* (Three jewels). These are right faith (*samyagdarśana*), right knowledge (*samyagjñāna*) and right conduct (*samyagcaritra*). All the three are essential for the attainment of *Mokṣa*, but Jainism gives primary importance to the third without which it is useless to observe the former two. Let us consider it in detail.

Jainism gives a long list of actions constituting the right conduct for a householder and for a monk separately. However, the *pañcamahāvratas* constitute the necessary ingredients of the conduct of everyone, whether a housholder or a monk. The *pañcamahāvratas* are: *ahiṃsā* (non-violence), *satya* (truthfulness), *asteya* (non-stealing), *brahmacarya* (celibacy) and *aparigraha* (non-attachment). It can be seen that these are essentially the same as the *pañcaśīla* of Buddhism (except perhaps the last one). *Ahiṃsā*, however, is given a very wide connotation in Jainism. Injury or harm caused to any living being in any form is *hiṃsā*. So *ahiṃsā* is to be practised not only in deed, but also in thought and words. Keeping ill will against anyone in thought or speaking harsh words to anyone is as good an example of *hiṃsā* as inflicting any bodily injury to anybody. Even forcing someone to do something against his will is *hiṃsā*. Similarly, causing injury to someone due to negligence is also *hiṃsā*. Practising *ahiṃsa* in the Jaina sense, therefore, is not very easy. It is a kind of *tapas*. To cultivate this virtue in its stringent spirit, the Jainas go to the extreme of not burning light or cooking meal after sunset, so that no worms could be attracted towards light and thereby killed. Jaina monks walk by brushing the path with a smooth brush in their hand so that no worm etc. should come under their feet.

It is not necessary to go into the details of other *vratas*, because they are well-known in both Hindu and Bauddha traditions. On the whole, they show non-attachment with the worldly objects to be a very important and essential ethical virtue. The same is the case with the Hindu and Bauddha traditions also. Besides the *mahāvratas*, Jainism prescribes many more *anuvratas* (supplementary norms) for a householder and still more for a monk. We cannot go into the details of those *anuvratas* here, but going through them will reveal that they are all norms concerning greater and greater purity, chastity, detachment, self-restraint, penance, renunciation etc. Thus, Jainism in line with Hinduism and Buddhism, rather in a more stringent manner, prescribes virtues meant for internal purity of the individual to lead him ultimately to *Mokṣa*. However, social virtues like love, compassion etc. are also not neglected. At least three of the *mahāvratas—ahiṃsā, satya* and *asteya*—and many within the *anuvratas* also show the direct concern of the Jainas for social virtues.

(g) *The Cārvāka*

Of the three heterodox systems, the remaining one, the Cārvāka system, is a Hindu system. In tune with Buddhism and Jainims it criticises the Vedic ritualism and ceremonialism. Rather, it is the most ardent and ruthless critic of the Vedas. In its ethical teachings it is equated with epicurianism and gross hedonism. According to it, to attain and enjoy maximum pleasure in this life is the only goal of man, because there is no other world or life beyond the present one. The Vedas have falsely and deceitfully shown the attraction of heaven for the attainment of which various kinds of rituals and sacrifices are prescribed. The Cārvākas make a fun of and ridicules all such Vedic prescriptions regarding rituals and sacrifices. According to them, these are all the innovations of the Brahmins to deceive people and to serve their own selfish ends.

However, this purely materialistic, hedonistic and anti-Vedic doctrine of the Cārvākas had very little impact on the general spiritualistic trend of the Hindu ethical ideas. It really never had any recognisable effect on the moral thinking of the Indian people. It simply shows that there is an example of purely materialistic Hindu thought also amidst the general spiritualistic trend of thought all over.

6. Modern Indian Thought

As we have seen earlier, the critics of Indian ethics have so often pointed towards its following weaknesses: (a) it is based more on authority for its source than on individual conscience or reasoning; (b) social morality has little place in it, because it mostly emphasises virtues of individual purity and restranit as moral virtues; (c) morality has only a subsidiary place in the final scheme of life, because only up to a certain stage it helps towards the attainment of liberation. After that it is to be given up in favour of the higher spiritual paths such as those of *dhyāna*, *sādhanā* or *samādhi*. As Mckenzie remarks, "...... 'dharma' has to do with a lower sphere of experience. It serves as a sort of platform over which one may climb to a position from which it becomes easier to reach the higher, but when this position has been reached, it is no longer needed."[32] It is not, however, a place to consider the justifibility of these criticisms.

Modern Indian thinkers, while propounding their ethical views, seem to have kept these criticisms seriously in their minds. They have tried to put their views across in a manner appropriate to hold aloft the modern Indian ethical thought without the stings of criticism appearing to have any worth. That the role of authority is the primary source of moral ideas and beliefs has not been generally denied by the modern Indian thinkers. They have also emphasized the role of individual conscience and reasoning in it. Some of them, for example, Sri Aurobindo and Radhakrishnan, have laid stress on the role of personal intuition or consceince in morality. Sri Aurobindo is very clear in this respect, as may be seen from his statement in this connection quoted in Chapter II. However, Indian thought in no phase of its development has taken individual reasoning to be the sole or even the principal guide and source of morality. The injunctions and prohibitions of the Śāstras and the counsels given by such personalities who have led a morally pure and elevated life have always been accorded primary importance in matters of morality. The inner voice of conscience, however, has never been neglected.

Social morality in Indian ethical thought is not less important. It is a bit biased to think that the ancient Indian thought has neglected the role of social morality. Even if the charge is somehow tenable so far as ancient Indian thought is concerned, it is hardly applicable to the Modern Indian thought. Almost all modern Indian thinkers, amongst whom special mention may be made of Vivekananda, Gandhi and Tagore, have emphasized the role of virtues and duties related to social morality. The virtues like love, compassion, universal brotherhood etc. have been repeatedly emphasized by these thinkers. As a matter of fact, modern Indian thought is humanistic in its approach and naturally the role of human virtues as mentioned above has been stressed. It is humanistic to the extent that even in matters of *Mokṣa*, it lays greater stress upon the desirability of universal salvation rather than that of individual salvation. Salvation is not complete until each and every individual is liberated.

Radhakrishnan and Sri Aurobindo explicitly project their ideas of universal salvation. Such a concept in one form or other is also present in the ideas of Vivekananda, Gandhi and Tagore.

The last criticism about the Indian ethical thought is completely unfounded in the light of the views of modern Indian thinkers. Barring Sri Aurobindo and Radhakrishnan, all other modern Indian thinkers have taken morality by itself as sufficient for leading to the goal of *Mokṣa*. They conceive *Mokṣa* in such a manner that the pursuit of humanistic virtues becomes relevant in its attainment. *Mokṣa* is nothing but the universalization of one's individualistic personality. This is, as Tagore says, nothing but realising oneself into others and others into oneself. This can be possible only by a true love for others.

So, true love becomes the most effective means for salvation. How can then it be said that in the ultimate scheme of life morality has been given a subsidiary place in Indian thought? Tagore is very explicit in emphasizing that it is only by living in this world and acting for others that one can attain his liberation. As he says, "He who thinks to reach God by running away from the world, when and where does he expect to meet him?"[33] Again, "A man must live the full term of his life and work without greed, and thus realize himself in the being who is in all beings. This means that he must reveal in his own personality the Supreme Person by his disinterested activities."[34]

Similarly, Gandhi has also laid stress on the fact that there is no greater religion than service of the suffering humanity. He has, more or less, identified the social ideal of *Sarvodaya* with the spiritual ideal of *Mokṣa*, implying thereby that one can attain his salvation only by working for the uplift of others. Salvation is self-realisation and self-realisation is nothing other than the realisation of the fundamental unity of one's own self with all other selves. And it is the self-same kind of realisation which is fulfilled in *Sarvodaya*. Hence, according to Gandhi, the spiritual ideal of self-realisation and social ideal of *Sarvodaya* are essentially the same. As the latter is attainable only by adopting the path of love, compassion and social service, so the former also is attainable by the self-same means.

Sri Aurobindo and Radhakrishnan, among modern Indian thinkers, have not attached ultimate value to ethical pursuits in the attainment of liberation. Radhakrishnan is a loyal Advaitin and it is quite natural for him to give *jñāna* the ultimate significance in this regard. Yet, he never ignores moral qualities such as those of self-sacrifice, love etc. in taking man to a significantly high level on the road to liberation. He firmly, believes in the desirability of the performance of actions for the benefit and help of others even by a liberated man. The only fact to be understood is that the moral actions at this stage are not done under any stress, rather they follow automatically and spontaneously out of the very nature of the liberated man. Similar views are of Sri Aurobindo also. He does not deny the significance of moral life in leading man to the divinisation of his being. What he wants to emphasize, however, is that true morality follows out of the nature of a man only when he is fully spiritualised and divinised. Morality then does not remain to be done under external considerations; it becomes the very nature of man. These things may be more clearly put here in his own words, "When the being of the man undergoes this transformation, then it is not his actions that standardise his nature, but his nature that gives value to his actions, then he is no longer laboriously virtuous, artificially moral, but naturally divine."[35]

But above all, I fail to understand why the Westerners so often complain that in Indian thought morality is not accorded the utmost significance in the scheme of life here. Such a complaint implies that the Indian system should assert the observance of morality as the only way to attain the highest goal of life. Such an assumption is obviously one-sided and wrong. Indian thinkers are more realistic and scientific in their approach when they accept that men in the world maybe, and actually are, of different temperaments and therefore one and only path (the moral path or the path of action) may not be suitable for all of them for attaining their goals. Therefore, they have spoken of alternative paths out of which one can adopt any one in accordance with his temperament.

And, moreover, the alternative paths are not exclusive to each other. Rather they are co-operative and supplementary and, really speaking, in the honest adoption of any one, all otheres are automatically realised and observed. Even in the adoption of the yogic path, the first few steps consist in the pursuit and observance of moral virtues, both social and individual. Almost all such systems also which have taken the path of knowledge as the path of *Mokṣa* do not neglect humanistic virtues. They only say that after a certain stage morality may be taken as having played its role in one's life and some more effective path, such as, *dhyāna, samādhi* etc. should be taken up for a speedy realisation of the goal.

After all, life is a staircase. It goes through stages, and different things may have their roles at different stages. Radhakrishnan very aptly says here, "Life is a staircase with steps leading to a goal . . . . growth is ordinarily gradual. Nature cannot be rushed."[36] The Indian theory of *Puruṣārthas* also teaches the same lesson. Why should we assume then that one and only one thing should have its role in our life from beginning to end? Morality is given its due place and then passed over. What is the harm in it? How is the status of morality lowered thereby? And above all, at no stage of man's development moral actions, specially those which are connected with human service, love etc. are prohibited in Indian thought. After the attainment of liberation (many Indain systems believe in *Jīvana mukti*) it is advised that the acts of human service should be continued with a pure sense of love for others. There is no need of any such advice also. By his very nature the liberated man becomes disposed to perform humanitarian duties. Morality becomes his nature. In Indian thought this is not a matter of mere theory, Lord Buddha and Mahāvīra provide outstanding examples.

REFERENCES

1. E.W. Hopkins, *Ethics of India* (New Heaven, Yale Univ. Press, 1924), p. 43:
2. Bloomfield, *Religion of the Vedas* (Indological Book House, Delhi, 1972), p. 125.
3. *Śatapatha Brāhmaṇa* X.2.3.6.
4. E.W. Hopkins, *Religions of India* (Ginn and Company, 1895), p. 84.
5. *Kaṭha Up.* I.2.24.
6. *Bṛh. Up.* 4.4.23.
7. *Taitt. Up.* 1.11.1.
8. Surama Dasgupta, *Development of Moral Philosophy in India* (Orient Long Mans, 1961), p. 70.
9. *Taitt. Up.* 1.11.3.
10. Surama Dasgupta, *op. cit.*, p. 13.
11. John Mckenzie, *op. cit.*, p. 54.
12. *Gautama* 1.8.22.
13. *Ibid.*, 1.824.
14. John Mckenzie, *op. cit.*, p. 64.
15. *Vasiṣṭha* VI.2-4
16. Surama Dasgupta, *op.cit.*, p. 25.
17. *BG.* II.42.
18. *Ibid.*, XVII.17-19.
19. *Ibid.*, XVII.14-16.
20. *Ibid.*, XVII.11-13.
21. *Ibid.*, XVII.20-22.
22. *Padārthadharmasaṃgraha* VI.133.
23. *SB* III.4.27.
24. S. Radhakrishnan, *The Vedānta* (Allen and Unwin, 1928), p. 188.
25. S.K. Maitra, *op. cit.*, p. 22 f.
26. *RB* 1.1.1.
27. *Ibid.*
28. Rāmānuja, *Gītābhāṣya* III.19-20.

29. John Mckenzie, *op. cit.*, p. 100
30. John Mckenzie, *op. cit.*, pp. 106-7.
31. S. Tachibana, *op. cit.*, p. 95.
32. John Mckenzie, *op. cit.*, p. 207.
33. R.N. Tagore, *Sādhanā*, p. 130.
34. R.N. Tagore, *The Religion of Man*, p. 118.
35. Sri Aurobindo, *op. cit.*, p. 204.
36. S. Radhakrishana, *Eastern Religions* etc., p. 366.

CHAPTER VII

Teleological and Deontological Theories in Indian Ethics

1. Teleology and Deontology: General Introduction

There are two types of theories in ethics in consequence of two types of anwers to the question: 'On what standard or criterion do we judge an action to be right or wrong or a trait or character to be virtuous or vicious?'. We call an action right or wrong and a character virtuous or vicious, but on what ground, on what criterion? Broadly speaking, there are two types of answers to this question. One type refers to some ulterior, non-moral end in reference to which an action is to be judged right or wrong. According to this type, an action is to be judged right if it leads to or helps in leading to a particular non-moral goal or end and an action is wrong if it does not lead to the goal or hinders in that respect. The rightness or wrongness of an action is determined with reference to its conduciveness or unconduciveness to a pre-accepted non-moral goal. The theory of ethics based on answer of this type is known as the teleological theory.

The other type does not refer to any ulterior non-moral end or goal. According to it, an action is right or wrong in virtue of its own merit or demerit and not in terms of the goal that it leads or does not lead to. An action is right or wrong simply because it is or its not in conformity with some moral rule, or because of some other considerations, but surely not because it either leads to or does not lead to a desired goal. The theory of ethics based on answer of the above kind is known as the deontological theory. William Frankena, while making distinction between the teleological and deontological theories, says, ".... for a teleologist the moral quality or value of actions, persons, or traits of character is dependent on the comparative non-moral value of what they bring about or try to bring about. Teleological theories, then, make the right, the obligatory, and the morally good dependent on the non-morally good...." In order to know whether something is right, ought to be done, or is morally good, one must first know what is good in the non-moral sense and whether the thing in question promotes or is intended to promote what is good in this sense.

Deontological theories deny what teleological theories affirm. They deny that the right, the obligatory and the morally good are wholly, whether, directly or indirectly, a function of what is nonmorally good .... They assert that there are other considerations that may make an action or rule right or obligatory besides the goodness or badness of its consequences—certain features of the act itself other than value it brings into existence, for example, the fact that it keeps a promise, is just, or is commanded by God or State. Teleologists believe that there is one and only one basic or ultimate right-making characteristic, namely the comparative value (non-moral) of what is, probably will be, or is intended to be brought into being. Deontologists either deny that this characteristic is right making at all or they insist that there are other basic or ultimate right making characteristics as well."[1]

It is clear from the above that for a teleological theory conduciveness to some goal is the necessary criterion for the rightness of an action whereas for a deontological theory either it is not at all the case or at least it is not the only and exclusive criterion for judging an action to be right; there are also other considerations besides. Now let us try to categorise the Indian theories of moral obligation and value as teleological and deontological on the basis of the above clarifications regarding the nature of the two theories.

2. The General Character of Indian Ethical System

At the first sight it appears that Indian ethics as a whole is to be characterised as teleological and there is no question of categorising it into teleological and deontological. The obvious reason is that almost all the views take *Mokṣa* to be the highest ideal of life, and morality (*dharma*) is a means to it. But it will be wrong to characterise all the views as teleological on this account. The mere fact that moral actions lead one to a non-moral goal does not make a theory teleological. Kant also accepted that morality is ultimately rewarded by happiness, but then he never took the conduciveness to happiness as the criterion of morality. An action was moral, according to him, simply because it was in accordance with the law of reason, and not because it led to happiness or any other such goal. Similarly, it is one thing to say that morality leads to *Mokṣa*, but quite another thing to say that only moral action leads to *Mokṣa*, or that conduciveness to *Mokṣa* is the criterion of any virtuous, right or moral action. There are systems of Indian thought which take

Mokṣa to be the highest end of life and also accept that moral actions lead to that goal but still do not regard some actions moral simply because they lead to *Mokṣa*. Rather, they regard that to be so on some other ground, such as, that it is according to the Śāstric law or that it is the law or will of God or some such other ground. So we will have to go into the details of the systems to see clearly which are actually teleological and which are not.

In a way the whole Indian ethical system is deontological. Something is *dharma* (duty, obligation or virtue) simply becasue it is a Vedic law or it is prescribed by Dharma Sūtras and Śāstras. This seems to be the temperament of the entire Indian system taken in general. We have seen definition of morality being advanced more often in terms of what is enjoined by the Vedas and the Dharma Śāstras. It is hardly said that what leads to *Mokṣa* is morality, but it is repeatedly said that what is enjoined by the Vedas, or what is willed by God or what marks the imitation of the virtues imbibed by God is morality. The Mīmāṃsā clearly says there is no duty other than what is prescribed by the Vedas. So, something is duty because it is enjoined by the Vedas as duty.

The characteristic deontological tone of Indian morlaity is very clearly reflected in the views of the *Mahābhārata*. The *Mahābhārata*, like Kant, recognises a relation between virtue and happiness. If the former does not lead to the latter, morality will be a hollow and insignificant affair. But then it adds that between virtue and happiness, the former is to be given preference, because conduciveness to the goal of happiness is not the criterion of virtue. In reply to Draupadī's sceptical reflections, Yudhiṣṭhira clearly sounds the following deontological note, "I never act solicitious of the fruits of my actions, O princess. I give away because it is my duty to give, I sacrifice because it is my duty to sacrifice. O Krishna, I accomplish to the best of my power whatever a person living in the domestic life should do, regardless of the fact whether those acts have fruits or not. I act virtuously, not from the desire of reaping fruits of virtue, but of not transgressing the ordinances of the Vedas, beholding the conduct of the good and the wise. My heart is naturally attracted towards virtue, O Krishna. The man who wisheth to reap the fruits of virtue is a trader in virtue. His nature is mean and he should never be counted among the virtuous:"[2]

> *"nāhaṃ dharmaphalākāṅkṣī rājaputrī carāmyutra,*
> *dadāmi deyamityeva yaje yaṣṭavyamityuta.*
> *astu vātra phalam mā vā kartavyaṃ puruṣeṇa yat,*

gṛhe nivasitā kṛṣṇe yathāsakti karomi tat.
dharmaṃ carāmi suśroṇi na dharmaphalakāraṇāta,
āgamānanatikramya satāṃ vṛttamavedṣya ca.
dharma evamanaḥ kṛṣṇe svabhāvāccaiva me dhṛtam,
dharma vāṇijyako hīno jaghanyo dharmavādinām."

Here the deontological nature of Indian ethics is quite clear. Duty is to be performed for duty's sake, virtue is to be inculcated because it is virtue, and not for achieving any end or goal. Something is obligatory not because it gives us something in return but simply because it is either the ordinance of the Veda or is followed by good and wise people.

The characteristic deontological tone of the *Bhagavadgītā,* which forms a part of the *Mahābhārata* itself, is quite well-known. The *Gītā* through its doctrine of *niṣkāma karma* advocates the doctrine of duty for duty's sake. The famous *Gītā* saying in this regard is as follows: "To action alone hast thou a right and never at all to its fruits; let not the fruits of actions be thy motive, neither let there be in thee any attachment to inaction."[3]

karmaṇyevādhikāraste mā phaleṣu kadācana,
mā karmaphalaheturbhūrmā te aṃgo'stvakarmaṇi.

Here *Gītā* clearly exhorts to act without any attachment or desire for *phala,* because *phala* is beyond our power. We have a right only to act, and not to hanker after fruits. The sanction for duty must come from within, and never from without. Duty is to be done only because it is duty and for no other consideration. The performance of duty will certainly bring its reward now or later, but that must not be the impelling force for the duty. The reward is not man's concern, that is rather God's concern. So man should perform his duty with sense of devotion without any concern for the result. The duties consist here of the duties related to one's *varṇa* and *āśrama* besides the various common or general duties known as *sādhāraṇa dharmas.* However, the *Gītā* lays emphasis on *svadharma* to put greater value to duties relative to one's *varṇa* and *āśrama.* If there is sometimes a conflict between the two kinds of duties —*sādhāraṇa* and *varṇāśrama*—perhaps the latter should prevail over the former according to the *Gītā.* This is clear from Lord Kṛṣṇa's advise to Arjuna in the battlefield. Even in spite of *ahiṃsā* being a *sādhāraṇa* or general moral duty, Kṛṣṇa advises Arjuna to perform the act of *hiṃsā* in the battlefield because it is his *svadharma,* his duty as a kṣatriya.

Nevertheless, all duties are to be performed devotedly with perfectly non-attached sense. The deontological tone is therefore quite clear.

One additional element to be noted in the above quoted *śloka* of the *Gītā* is that it is totally against inaction. Sometimes, a charge is levelled against Hinduism that it essentially teaches inaction. But such hostile charges are totally denied by the viewpoint of the *Gītā* as presented in the above *śloka*. *Gītā* prohibits attached actions as much as inaction. Action or activity is our nature. We should never try to avoid it. Actions we are to do, but only non-attached actions which do not bind.

Any way, the main question we must answer is: wherein lies the obligatoriness of our moral actions? or, in other words, where does the obligatoriness of our actions follow from? Does it follow from the end that our actions help to achieve or from the law or authority or something like that which dictates them? We are to perform moral duties, but for what? Are they to be performed for the reason that they lead to some ulterior end like *Mokṣa* or for the reason that they are dictated by some faithful and reverential authority? Almost all the Indian systems believe that the performance of moral actions leads to *Mokṣa,* if not directly, at least by facilitating the way for other effective means which directly leads to *Mokṣa.* But it is one thing to say that morality facilitates attaining *Mokṣa* and quite another to say that morality is to be followed because it leads to *Mokṣa*. In the latter case, the obligatoriness for morality follows from *Mokṣa* while in the former case it hardly so follows. So we have to see whether in every Indian system the obligatoriness for moral action comes from the highest end *Mokṣa.*

3. The Nyāya-Vaiśeṣika

In the Nyāya-Vaiśeṣika system the answer the above question seems to be in the affirmative. In the Vaiśeṣika sūtras, the very definition of *dharma* is given in terms of the ulterior ends like *abhyudaya* (prosperity) and *niḥśreyasa.* It is said that whatever leads to prosperity and highest end is *dharma* (*yato'bhyudayaniḥśreyasasiddhiḥ sa dharmaḥ* —V.S.1.2). So here it seems clear that the obligatoriness for *dharma* arises from the twin ends of worldly prosperity and final liberation. Some actions are to be called moral or immoral with reference to whether they lead to the twin ends or not. The Vaiśeṣika morality is definitely teleological then. Similarly, the Nyāya gives primary importance to *Iṣṭasādhanatā* in determining the obligatoriness of a moral action, or a moral law on which some action is based. In the words of Prof. S.K. Maitra, "The Naiyāyikas point out that the nature of moral obligation would be inexplicable without the concception of an end, good or *iṣṭa* to be attained, there being no discrimination possible between virtue (*dharma*) and vice (*adharma*) without such a conception."[4]

The Naiyāyikas, no doubt, believe in God and, according to them, it is God who is the author of the Vedic injunctions and prohibitions which form the basis of our moral duties (*dharma*). It should follow, therefore, from this that the ultimate obligatoriness of our duties comes from the authority of God and not from any *phala* or consequence of our actions. But this is not the case. In spite of taking God as the prime source of the moral imperative, the Naiyāyikas somehow tag the question of the obligatoriness of some action to its good or evil consequences. *Phalecchā* or *Iṣṭasādhanatā* becomes a necessary factor in determining the obligatoriness of an action. As Prof. S.K. Maitra explains the whole thing, "Scriptural imperatives are of course personal commands being the prescriptions of the Lord to imperfect beings. There is compulsion implied in such commands, but this is only because the Lord creates good and evil through His injunctions and prohibitions. Whatever the Lord commands is good and good because the Lord commands it. Similarly, whatever the Lord forbids is evil because the Lord forbids it. The authority of the scriptural prescriptions on the will of the agent is thus a *vyāpāra* or process in the agent himself: it is the desire for the good and aversion towards the evil involved in the injunctions and the prohibitions of scripture as the Lord's commands. It is these desires and aversions in the agent that are the real operative forces and moral authority is the operation of the good and the evil through the agent's subjective desires and aversions. Hence according to the Naiyāyikas *Vidhi* is a personal command which compels acceptance through *phalecchā* or desire for the consequence."[5] All this shows that according to the Nyāya system although the *Vidhi* (The Vedic injunctions) is God's command, its operation takes place through the agent's *phalechhā*, which, in the main, determines the obligatoriness of the action. The Nyāya-Vaiśeṣika thus seems to be a teleological moral system in which the end does not form only the motive for action but also the moral obligatoriness.

4. The Mīmāṃsā

As opposed to this, the Mīmāṃsakas do not take the obligatoriness of moral actions as stemming from the consequence or the end. According to Kumārila, the end or *phala* may be said to determine the motive of the agent, but not the obligatoriness. The obligatoriness is the result of the *Vidhi* of which the action in question is an instance. The imperativeness or the obligatoriness of the action is independent of the end or *phala*. To quote Professor Maitra again, "According to Kumārila, the end, the consequence determines only the motive or the choice, but not the obligatoriness of the imperative. . . . The *phala* or consequence is only *pravarttaka*, i.e. a psychological motive but is not *vidheya*, i.e. the object of moral imperative. It is a psychological implicate of the moral action, an end as motive being necessary for moral as for all actions, but it is not a moral implicate of the imperative which is obligatory independently of the end or consequence."[6] Hence, the end or *phala*, according to Kumārila, forms only the motive to move the agent for action. What makes the action moral or immoral is simply its Vedic sanction or lack of it. The moral obligatoriness of the action follows from the Vedic source without any consideration for the consequence.

In spite of Kumārila's view stated above, his view in relation to the *kāmya karmas* is not without discrepancy. For, in such actions, it is the agent's *kāmanā* or desire for fruit which is the reason of the imperative being carried and therefore in such cases the authority or the obligatoriness arises from the end or the consequence itself. But Kumārila will point out that the authority or obligatoriness is independent of the end even in case of *kāmya karmas*. Though the operation of the *Vidhi* takes place due to the *kāmanā* (for end), the obligatoriness of the action lies in the *Vidhi* itself. He would point out that there is an end, even in case of *nityanaimittika karmas*, known as unconditional or absolute duties. The end is the avoidance of sin which would accrue by the non-performance of the act. What refers to the end is only the agent's motive, not the authority or the obligatoriness of the duty. The authority or the obligatoriness arises from the law itself. In other words, although the performance of duty, *kāmya* or *nityanaimittika* will certainly bring certain consequences, these consequences form only the motive of the actions and not their authority or obligatoriness; the agent is to perform these duties simply for the reason that they are his duties. As says Prof. Maitra, "—The imperative would not have existed except for the *artha* or end to be realised by the act, but it does not derive its imperative character from the end. It has intrinsic, independent authority of its own. The end is thus a psychological implicate or accompaniment of the imperative, and does not constitute its moral authority."[7] Hence, it is clear that in the Kumārila Mīmāṃsā, as compared to the Nyāya, there is a definite transition from the consequential or teleological morality to deontological morality, although the latter has its purest form in yet another school of Mīmāṃsā which is represented by Prabhākara.

For Prabhākara, as Prof. Maitra says, "there is no extraneous end in the *Vidhi* as imperative, morally, psychologically or metaphysically. The imperative is its own end and constitutes the sanction, the motive as well as the moral authority of the *Vidhi*."[8] The *Vidhi* or the moral law thus constitutes its own end and does not imply any extreneous end or motive. Not only this, Prabhākara would maintain that in conceiving an external sanction for the moral imperative in the form of an end or *phala*, the Naiyāyikas fail to explain moral obligation. For this will lead according to Prabhākara to *anāvasthā* (infinite regress). The external end from which we think the moral authority flows must in its turn assume some other end to justify its authority. This other end again should assume yet another end to justify the authority of its own and the chain will go on and on endlessly. The Naiyāyikas can avoid this *anāvastha doṣa* only "by investing the external consequence with intrinsic independent authority."[9]

As regards the distinction between the *kāmya karmas* and the *nityanaimittika karmas* (conditional and unconditional duties) Prabhākara seems to hold that the former are not to be called moral actions proper. In such actions the imperative becomes *udāsīna* or morally neutral. In case of the *kāmya karmas* the function of the imperative is only to establish a relation between means and end, between the act and the consequence. Only unconditional duties are to be regarded as proper duties or as moral duties. In case of them the imperative is self-authoritative and self validating. The sanction is intrinsic without any reference to any extraneous end. In the words of Prof. Maitra, "In unconditional duty, the imperative is its own end and sanction and is thus self-authoritative or self-validating, while in *kāmya* actions it is without any imperative character, its function being merely to establish a relation of means and end between the act and the consequence desired to be attained thereby."[10] The Prabhākara Mīmāṃsā is thus definitely deontological in its tone and character.

5. The Rāmānuja Vedānta

The Viśiṣṭādvaita system of Rāmānuja also comes to be a deontological system on scrutiny insofar as its characterisation as a moral system is concerned. Like other Indian systems, the system of Rāmānuja also takes *Mokṣa* to be the ultimate human end. Furthermore, by virtue of believing in *samuccayavāda*. Rāmānuja gives morality an important place in men's effort for attaining *Mokṣa*. But the question is, does conduciveness to *Mokṣa* constitute the necessary condition for an action to be moral? Does the obligatoriness of a moral action follow from the final end *Mokṣa*? The answer is a clear 'no'. For the obligatoriness of moral actions in the system of Rāmānuja follows from the fact that moral qualities in their absolute and ultimate perfection constitute the essential nature of God and man's duty is simply to imitate or to follow those moral qualities. Thus man's moral virtues and duties are derivations from God's moral qualities. They are to be observed and followed simply because they represent God's qualities and God wants men to follow the moral qualities that He possesses in a perfect and absolute manner. So the sanction and authority of morality comes from no less a being than God. Moral qualities imbibed by God in a perfect manner are for us to imitate. In other words, our duty is to behave in a way God would do in a similar circumstance. For example, God possesses the moral quality of compassion, so we should be compassionate towards others; God possesses the quality of forgiveness, so we should forgive those who do wrong to us, and so on. In Rāmānuja's system God is regarded as a Moral Ideal with reference to which man's duties are to be derived or deduced. So man's moral duties follow directly from the moral perfections of God and not from any non-moral end like *Mokṣa*. So, Rāmānuja's system also is a deontological system and not a teleological one.

6. The Sāṃkhya and the Advaita Vedānta

In Sāṃkhya and Advaita Vedānta, as we have already seen, morality is neither necessary nor sufficient for *Mokṣa*. So the question of the obligatoriness of the moral actions following from this non-moral end perhaps does not arise. Nevertheless, none of the systems takes moral virtues and duties simply valueless. What Sāṃkhya criticises in the name of 'works' are mainly the ritualistic acts of the Vedas. But in its turn Sāṃkhya realises the importance of the moral virtues following from the *sāttvika* nature of man. These moral virtues pave to some extent one's path for *Mokṣa* also. But what is important to realise is that these moral virtues do not derive their sanction from end whether *Mokṣa* or anything else. They derive their sanction rather from the metaphysical nature of man.

Man as a psychophysical being is an evolute of Prakṛti. Of the three *guṇas* of Prakṛti, Sattva is the most commendable, because it is the repository of good human qualities. So virtues following from Sattva, such as, kindness, restraint of sense-organs etc., are to be inculcated and followed. Similarly, in Śaṃkara moral virtues do not derive their sanction from *Mokṣa*, although they serve as auxiliaries in the attainment of *Mokṣa*.

Here it may be mentioned that unlike Sāṃkhya, Śaṃkara gives some role to Vedic actions also including *āśrama dharma* etc., in making the path of *Mokṣa* somewhat smoother. But the main point for us to see here is that the sanction or authority of these acts does not lie in their being conducive to *Mokṣa*. The sanction lies in the Śāstras which enjoin performing various acts of rituals or actions according to *varṇa* and *āśrama*. The more refined human virtues like love and kindness have their sanction in the very nature of man.

Man as man is essentially soul, in which respect he is identical with *Brahman*, the fundamental reality. In essential nature, therefore, all human beings are one. Their difference is only apparent and external. So the moral virtues of love, kindness etc. automatically follow from the very metaphysical nature of man. Whatever role morality has to play in the systems of Sāṃkhya and Vedānta, it is essentially deontological morality. The morality or immorality of an action is determined not by its conduciveness or otherwise to some ulterior end, but by either its being enjoind by the Śāstras or its emerging spontaneously from the metaphysical nature of man.

7. The Non-orthodox Systems (Cārvāka, Buddhism and Jainism)

Of the three non-orthodox Indian systems, the Cārvāka (which is a Hindu system) is definitely a teleological system, because, according to it, the criterion for any action to be moral is the conduciveness of that action to worldly pleasure, a non-moral end. But the two non-Hindu systems—Bauddha and Jaina—are essentially deontological in nature. Like idealistic or spiritualistic Hindu systems they, no doubt, believe that performance of moral acts somehow contributes to the attainment of *Mokṣa*. In other words, we can say that both of these systems believe that moral actions definitely lead to desirable consequences in respect of both the worldly life and the life beyond. But the obligatoriness of moral actions or principles according to none of these systems flows from any extreneous end or goal. On the other hand, the obligatoriness flows from the venerable authority that is bestowed upon the original propounders of the two systems—Lord Buddha and Lord Mahāvīra.

In Buddhism, it is not the case that whatever leads to *Nirvāṇa* is *dharma*, rather whatever the Buddha has enjoined to observe and follow is *dharma*. It is a different matter that the observance of this *dharma* incidentally leads to *Nirvāṇa*. Similarly, in Jainism deeds coming under right action (*samyak caritra*) are to be followed along with right faith and right knowledge not for their conduciveness to *Kaivalya*, but for their being enjoined upon us by the great *Tīrthaṅkara* Lord Mahāvīra. So, sanction of moral actions lies in their sources, and not in the end that they lead to. Hence, we can see that both Buddhism and Jainism in their essential spirit are also deontological moral systems.

Thus despite *Mokṣa* being the ultimate human end towards which all philosophical, religious and moral efforts are supposed to be directed in the Indian tradition, the Indian moral system, by and large, proves to be deontological in nature. And it is quite natural for it to be so. We have seen that the Śāstras have been regarded as the primary source and sanction of *dharma* in India. That implies that although the observance of the Śāstric *dharmas* naturally and undoubtedly leads to good consequences, their moral worth is not to be evaluated in terms of the consequences. Their moral worth is to be determined and assessed only with reference to whether they are enjoined by the Śāstras. In other words, *dharma* is *dharma* not because it leads to *Mokṣa,* but because it has been enjoined by authority to be *dharma*. Hence, clearly the overall tone of Indian morality is deontological, implying thereby that *dharma* is to be followed for the reason that it is *dharma* as enjoined by authority.

REFERENCES

1. W.K. Frankena, *Ethics*, pp. 14-15.
2. *The Mahābhārata*, Vana Parva, 31. 2-6.
3. *BG* II.47.
4. S.K. Maitra, *op. cit.*, p. 126.
5. *Ibid.*, pp. 119-20.
6. *Ibid.*, pp. 126-127.
7. *Ibid.*, p. 128.
8. *Ibid.*, p. 129.
9. *Ibid.*, p. 129.
10. *Ibid.*, p. 131.

CHAPTER VIII

The Content of Dharma: Virtues and Duties

1. The Concepts of Virtue and Duty

Virtues and duties are logically separate categories. While virtues are certain dispositions, attributes of character, inner traits, duties are overt acts to be performed either in pursuance of certain laws prescribed by some authority or for the attainment of some desirable goal. While charity, good deed, serving the distressed, reading of scriptures (may be called religious duty rather than moral duty proper, but duty nonetheless) are duties, benevolence, love modesty, forgiveness are virtues. On the practical plane, a sharp line of distinction between the two may not always be possible because they are intimately related with each other.

To say that compassion or kindness is a virtue is, more or less, the same as saying that it is our duty to be compassionate towards others. Similarly, to say that it is our moral duty to forgive others is the same as saying that forgiveness is a moral virtue. It is very difficult, therefore, to draw a sharp line of distinction between virtues and duties on the practical plane. Whether morality consists in the mere performance of certain specific duties or manifests in certain inner traits of our character is sometimes open to controversy. In other words, the controversy is whether we are to follow the morality of doing or of being. Generally, consensus is in favour of the morality of being because without inner roots of virtuous character mere mechanical doing of acts will not make one moral. Leslie Stephen has expressed the idea in the following words: ". . . . morality is internal. The moral law has to be expressed in the form 'be this', not in the form 'do this'.[1] But it can be seen that this controversy is futile. A virtuous character without actual doing of virtuous deeds is morally as useless as a good deed done without a pure inner root of character. Morality really must incorporate both of these. Speaking, more or less, in the Kantian style, Frankena expresses the intimate relationship between the morality of doing and that of being in the following words: ". . . .principles without traits are impotent and traits without principles are blind."[2]

The intimate relationship between virtues and duties has led Indian thinkers to employ the term '*dharma*' to denote both and has prevented them from giving sharply distinguished lists of virtues and duties. Writers on Indian ethics, such as Prof. S.K. Maitra, have tried to present separately classified lists of virtues and duties credited to ancient Indian moral thinkers such as Manu and Praśastapāda. It is not clear how what have been put under 'virtues' will be justified as pure virtues sharply distinguished from duties, and those listed 'duties' as pure duties sharply distinguish able from virtues. For example, the list of ten *sādhāraṇa dharmas* (*dhṛti, kṣamā* etc.) as given by Manu has been characterised by Maitra as a list of duties. A perusal of these reveals that most of them are, strictly speaking, virtues, rather than duties. Even the original texts, and not only the interpreters like Maitra, raise such confusion. For example, in the Bhagavadgītā, the following have been enumerated as the *karmas* (Dr. Radhakrishnan has interpreted the term 'karma' as 'duty') of Brahmin: self-control, austerity, purity, forbearance, uprightness, wisdom, knowledge and faith in religion. We may see that most, rather all, of these are virtues rather than duties. So, one may say that there has been in Indian moral thought an overall confusion regarding the distinction between virtues and duties. Or, we should say that Indian thinkers well-realised that such a distinction in a sharp manner could not be made and therefore they did not bother much about the distinction. On a conceptual plane, such a distinction may be made, although one must always have to remember that in talking about virtues one can not separate the correlated duties. The same thing happens to duties in being mixed with correlated virtues.

2. Virtues and Duties in Indian Ethics

Some virtues like compassion, forgiveness, freedom from covetousness, freedom from anger, truth, non-violence, control of senses etc. have always been emphasized. Similarly, some duties like charity or liberality (*dāna*), doing good to others, sacrifice, *tapas* etc. have so often been talked about and stressed upon. But the most frequently repeated list of virtues or duties (*dharma*) that we come across in the Indian tradition, including the Hindu, Jain and Bauddha traditions, is the following: *satya* (truth), *ahiṃsā* (non-violence), *brahmacarya* (celibacy), *asteya* (non-stealing) and *aparigraha* (non-attachment). These five constitute the five *yamas* of Hindu tradition, the *pañcamahāvrata* of the Jaina tradition and *pañcaśīla* of the Buddhist tradition. Notwithstanding differences about the connotation in the three traditions, they refer more or less to the same traits of character and conduct. *Satya* refers to being veracious in thought, speech and action—all the three. *Ahiṃsā* refers not only to overt non-killing of living beings, but also to non-harming or non-injuring any creature in any way. More often than not, it carries with it the positive trait of love, kindness etc. also. *Brahmacàrya* generally refers to a control over all the sense-organs, but more specifically it refers to the control of sex-drive. *Asteya* is non-stealing of the property of others. But *asteya* prohibits not only actual stealing, it also prohibits entertaining any thought of taking away what belongs to others. Sometimes, *asteya* is given such a wide connotation that it comes very near to *aparigraha*, which means non-attachment to worldly objects.

The above list contains virtues and duties. Truth, non-violence and non-stealing may be regarded as duties, while celibacy and non-attachment as virtues. But in a sense all of them may be regarded as virtues—virtues of self-restraint. Some refer to social morality, while others to individual morality. Truth, non-violence and non-stealing have obvious social implications, while celibacy and non-attachment have primary reference to self-control.

(a) *The Vedas and the Upaniṣads*

A detailed idea of the virtues and duties recognised in Indian moral tradition can be had from the lists presented from time to time by various moralists or moral thinkers. The enumeration of the qualities of character and conduct actually begins from the Vedas and Upaniṣads themselves although generally speaking, the former is regarded as a treatise on rituals and the latter on *jñāna*. We have seen in our sixth chapter that in spite of being in one sense volumes on rituals and *jñāna* respectively, the Vedas and the Upaniṣads have not failed recognising the important role that moral virtues and duties play in lifting the man to his spiritual destiny. We have also seen there that the most emphasised virtues (or duties) in the Vedas are: *satya, tapas, yajña brahamcarya, śraddhā, dāna* etc. Besides these, friendship, hospitality, non-cheating and non-violence also get important place in the Vedas. The vices condemned are lying, gambling, arrogance etc. The Upaniṣads also emphasize the Vedic virtues like *satya, tapas, yajña, dāna,* but give wider connotations to the latter three. Besides, they also lay emphsis on such qualities of character and conduct as study of the Vedas, compassion, self-control, right dealing etc.

(b) ***The Dharma-sūtras and the Dharmaśāstras (Sādhāraṇa Dharmas)***

Various virtues and duties pertaining to actual life of an Indian may be found in the Dharma-sūtras and Dharma-śāstras. Man's *dharmas*, on the whole, are divided herein into *sādhāraṇa* and *Varṇāśrama dharmas*. The former refer to the *dharmas* of man in general, while the latter refer to the *dharmas* of man in relation to the *varṇa* (class) or *āśrama* (stage of life) he belongs to. The most popularly recognised list of *sādhāraṇa dharmas* is that of Manu (*dhṛti, kṣamā* etc.) which we have already seen in our Chapter VI. It can be well-seen from the list that almost all are, strictly speaking, virtues rather than duties. This can also be seen that the virtues enumerated mostly relate to individual's self-culture or self-discipline, although some like *kṣamā, asteya, akrodha* and *satya* have got a social reference also. However, as Maitra perhaps rightly points out, the above virtues are only negatively related to society because in place of recommending positive duties of social service they advise restraint in relation to society. Maitra's remark in this connection is as follows: "There is practically no recognition of social duties proper, i.e. of the duties of social service in a positive sense as distinguished from negative toleration (*kṣamā*) and non-appropriation (*cauryābhāva*). Even veracity does not necessarily imply positive social service in this sense: it aims at negative non-interference rather than positive service and it may be practised purely as a dianoetic virtue of self-culture. . ."[3] However, at other places Manu also speaks of other virtues[4] like *akārpaṇya* (liberality), hospitality and non-violence in which we can mark Manu's concern for positive social virtues. In general, however, we can say that the virtues enumerated by Manu relate both to individual and social morality, the former gaining greater importance.

A more exhaustive list of *dharmas* having both social and individual implications may be found in Āpastamba. Āpastamba first gives a list of vices, and then in contrast, a list of virtues. The vices include: anger, exultation (*harṣa*), grumbling (*roṣa*), covetousness, delusion, ostentation (*dambha*), malice (*droha*), untruth, excessive eating, false accusation upon other, envy, lust (*kāma*), secret hatred, neglect to keep the senses in subjection (*anātmyam*), neglect to concentrate the mind (*ayogaḥ*).[5] The virtues, in contrast, are as follows: freedom from anger, freedom from exultation, freedom from grumbling, freedom from covetousness, freedom from delusion, freedom from ostentation, freedom from malice, truthfulness, moderation in eating, abstention from accusing others, non-enviousness, self-denying liberality (*samvibhāgastyāga*), avoiding to accept gifts, uprightness, affability, extinction of passions, subjection of senses, peace with with all created beings (*sarvabhutairvirodho*), concentration of the mind, regulation of conduct according to the Aryan rules, absence of cruelty, and contentment.[6]

It is said that those who follow these virtues attain the Cosmic Soul (*Viśvātmā*). This indicates a firm belief in the efficacy of moral path in leading to the highest destiny. A glance over the list of vices and virtues can bring out their relation both to individual and social morality. Some virtues like self-denying liberality, peace with all creatures, abstention from accusing others have definitely a social reference. Most of the virtues, however, are meant for self-control and self-purification. The vice and virtue of excessive and moderate eating respectively have no connection with morality whatsoever. It has been included, perhaps, with the idea that moderation in eating helps maintaining a good mental condition so very necessary in cultivating self-purifying virtues like subjection of senses, concentration of mind etc. Such virtues with seemingly no connection with morality can be seen included in the Indian list of virtues. The explanation for this may be found in the recognition of individual morality by Indian thinkers. Individual morality has for its essence self-purification and many virtues, purely hygienic or intellectual (like Manu's *dhi* and *vidyā*) or something like that make significant contribution in the attainment of self-purification.

An important feature of Āpastamba's list is the enumeration of both vices and virtues. Most virtues stand in contrast to the vices enumerated, but some additional or independent virtues like avoiding acceptance of gifts, promotion of peace with all creatures, regulation of conduct according to the Aryan rules, uprightness, affability etc. are also included. Again, secret hatred is a vice to which no corresponding virtue is mentioned in contrast. Most of the virtues, again, have negative import implying thereby that they are meant more for self-restraint and self-control than for positive social effects.

Gautama lists eight good qualities of soul (virtues) which are already mentioned in Chapter VI. The distinguishing feature of Gautama's list is that it starts from a very important social virtue, *dayāsarvabhūteṣu* (compassion on all creatures). Most of the other listed virtues, some of which are common with either Manu's or Āpastamba's, are those relating to individual morality mainly aiming at self-purification.

Similar lists of generic virtues may be cited from other Dharmasūtras like that of Yājñavalkya, but it is no use citing more or less similar virtues. The above lists from Manu, Āpastamba and Gautama give a general idea of the kinds of virtues which have been emphasised by the

Dharmasūtras and Dharmaśāstras. We will better present here the *Bhagavadgītā* list of generic virtues which includes within it almost all the virtues which have been enumerated in the Vedas and Upaniṣads as well as in the Dharmasūtras and Dharmaśāstras. According to the *Bhagavadgītā,* fearlessness, purity of mind, wise apportionment of knowledge and concentration (*Jñāna yogavyavasthitiḥ*) charity (*dāna*), self-control (*dama*), sacrifice (*yajña*), study of scriptures, austerity (*tapas*), uprightness (*ārjava*), non-violence, truth, freedom from anger, renunciation, tranquillity, aversion to fault finding, compassion to living beings, freedom from covetousness, gentleness, modesty, steadiness (*acapalam*) vigour, forgiveness, fortitude, purity (*śaucam*), freedom from malice (*adroha*) and freedom from excessive pride (*nātimānitā*) are the endowments of a person born with the divine nature.[7] According to the Gītā, these are the qualities of good man. We can very well mark that the list contains almost all the virtues recognised in the Vedic and Upaniṣadic traditions as well as in the Dharmasūtras and Dharmaśāstra. The virtues, once again therefore, are mostly of the nature of individual self-control, self-discipline and self-purification, although a few have social implications too.

(c) *The Nyāya-Vaiśeṣika (Sāmānya or Sādhāraṇa Dharmas)*

When we come to the systems, we find two important lists of *sāmānya dharmas*—one presented by Praśastapāda in the Vaiśeṣika tradition and another presented by Vātsyāyana in the Nyāya tradition. Praśastapāda presents the following list: regard for *dharma* (*dharma śraddhā*), non-injury, seeking the good of creatures (*bhūtahitatva*), truthfulness, non-stealing, celibacy (*brahmacarya*), purity of motive (*anupadhā*), restraint of anger (*krodhavarjana*), cleanliness (*abhiṣecana*), eating of pure food, devotion to the recognised deity (*viśiṣṭa devatā bhakti*), fasting and moral watchfulness (*apramāda*). It can be seen that in this list some of the virtues or duties are, generally speaking, of a religious or sacramental nature and some are hygienic. They may, in a sense, be taken as elements of individual morality. Most of the virtues, however, are obviously moral. The addition of *bhūtahitatva* speaks clearly of Praśastapāda's concern for social virtues. Again, the addition of virtues like regard for *dharma,* purity of motive and moral watchfulness is very significant from the moral point of view. Some purely intellectual virtues like wisdom and learning, as we find in Manu's list, have been removed and a fresh one—fasting—has been added. It seems fasting as a virtue has been first recognised by Praśastapāda. It may be a matter of dispute how far fasting can be regarded as a moral virtue. It is to be regarded, perhaps, more as a religious or hygienic virtue than as a moral one. But it has gained a significant place as virtue in the Jaina tradition. It has acquired much popularity in the Hinduism too as a religious virtue. Gandhijee used it extensively as a self-purifying practice and also as a means of creating mass impact for removal of many social evils.

Vātsyāyana classifies *dharma* according to the faculties involved in the exercise of the virtue or duty concerned. According to him, a *dharma* may be related to body (*kāyika*) or to speech (*vācika*) or again to mind (*mānasika*). Similarly, there can be corresponding vices relating to all the three. Vātsyāyana presents a list of both virtues and vices relating to all the three faculties. Virtues relating to body are according to him: *Paritrāṇa* (serving or saving the distressed), *dāna* (charity), and *paricaraṇa* (social service). Virtues relating to speech are: *satya* (truthfulness), *priyavacan* (agreeable speech), *hitavacana* (benificient speech) and *svādhyāya* (reading of scriptures). Virtues relating to the mind are: *dayā* (kindness) *aspṛhā* (non-covetousness or non-attachment) and *śraddhā* (reverence or piety). The corresponding vices are the following. Vices relating to body: *hiṃsā* (violence), *steya* (stealing) and *pratisiddha maithun* (prohibited sexual intercourse). Vices relating to speech: *mithyā vacana* (false speech), *paruṣa vacana* (harsh speech), *sūcanā* (insinuation) and *asambaddha* (gossip). Vices relating to mind: *paradroha* (hostility), *paradravyābhipsā* (covetousness for others' belongings) and *nāstikya* (want of faith in scriptures).

The mix up between virtues and duties (or between vices and wrong doings) may be clearly seen in the list. However, enough attention seems to be given here on *dharmas* relating to society. *Paritrāṇa, dāna, paricaraṇa, dayā, priyavacana, hitavacana* are all social *dharmas*. Thus, the primary character of the classification lies in its social orientation. Virtues or duties recognised generally as religious are also not wanting. The vices enumerated in correspondence with the virtues fit in suitably with each other except one: it is not very clear how *pratisiddha maithuna* is opposite to social service. However, Maitra's comment may be somewhat useful on the point, "It may be said, however, that just as *paricaraṇa* consists in doing good to society, so *pratisiddha maithuna* ends the social fabric by loosening the social bond and weakening the stock."[8] To many, the explanation may appear to be strained and farfetched.

(d) *The Yoga*

Patañjali presents yet another classification of the general virtues and duties to be followed by each and everyone desirous of attaining the highest destiny. They are in the form of five restraints (*yamas*) and five positive rules of character and conduct (*niyamas*). The *yamas* are already mentioned towards the beginning of this chapter. The *niyamas* are: *śauca* (cleanliness) or purity, *santoṣa* (contentment), *tapas, svādhyāya* (reading of scriptures) and *Īśvaraprāṇidhāna* (meditation on the glory and perfection of God). From the nomenclatures it seems the *yamas* are purely negative in implication while the *niyamas* are positive applications. But the way in which Patañjali interprets the *yamas* gives them much of positive contents. They hardly remain counsels for mere abstentions, rather they lead to certain positive virtues or duties also. For example, non-violence leads to kindness, sympathy, love etc., which are all positive virtues. Similarly, truthfulness is not merely avoidance of falsehood, rather it consists in positive truth-speaking. *Brahmacarya* is not only restraint on sex-organ or even on general sense-organs, it is rather the positive virtue of regulating the senses towards right direction. *Asteya* and *aparigraha* are, of course, predominantly virtues of restraint, but they are also not purely negative in implication. They are rather counsels for developing a positive attitude of detraction and indifference towards worldly objects, so that mind could be engaged towards higher spiritual pursuits. Both the *yamas* and the *niyamas* contain virtues and duties together. Amongst the *niyamas*, contentment alone can be regarded as virtue proper, rest are duties of which the last one may be regarded as a religious duty. In the system of Patañjali, however, it may be regarded as an element of individual morality. The *niyamas* are all, except perhaps *santoṣa*, positive doings. None of the *yamas* or *niyamas* is an absolutely new addition. We have found each one of them mentioned in some or other previous lists.

(e) *The Rāmānuja Vedānta*

Rāmānuja, like others, also lists certain essential virtues to be inculcated and followed by men, but his list has a speciality of its own. In the Indian tradition there are thinkers or systems who preach certain virtues which can, strictly speaking, be called religious. Rāmānuja preaches a morality in general which may very well be characterised as religious morality. He takes God as a paradigm of excellent moral qualities. Man's duty, according to him, is simply to imitate these qualities with utmost faith and sincerity. The excellent qualities in God are: *Jñāna* (knowledge), *kṣamā* (forgiveness), *śakti* (might), *kṛpā* (kindness), *vātsalya* (tenderness), *śīla* (humility), *ārjava* (uprightness), *sauhārda* (sympathy) and *mārdava* (gentleness). Man is expected to inculcate these virtues possessed by God in a paradigmatic manner. But there is again speciality in Rāmānuja's counsel. The virtues are specifically to be directed towards those who lack in them. For example, sympathy is to be directed towards the wicked in heart, because he lacks in this quality. Similarly, *śakti* is to be directed towards the weak for helping him (*śakti aśaktānām*), kindness is to be extended towards the distressed (*kṛpā dukhinām*), humility to the arrogant (*śīlam mandanām*), uprightness to the crooked (*ārjavam kutilānām*) and so on.

3. Varṇāśrama Dharmas

The various virtues and duties that man in general is advised to cultivate and follow come under the *sāmānya* or *sādhāraṇa dharmas*. They are *sāmānya* (general) in the sense that they are expected to be inculcated and followed by every man, irrespective of the class or stage of life he belongs to. But, as is well-known, Hinduism divides society into four classes and every individual's life span into four stages. Consequently, it prescribes specific duties relative to each class and stage of life. Although the reference to the four classes is first to be found in the *Ṛg Veda* itself, it is the Smṛti literature which elaborately deals with their specific qualities and duties. Besides the *Dharmasūtras, Dharmaśāstras* and the *Bhagavadgītā*, Praśastapāda also deals with the qualities and duties relative to each *varṇa* and *āśrama* in a detailed manner. Based on the various literatures of the Indian tradition, the following are the qualities/duties relative to each *varṇa* and *āśrama:*

A. *Varṇa Dharma:*

1. *Qualities and duties of a Brahmin:*
   - (a) Qualities—serenity (*śama*), self-control (*dama*), austerity (*tapas*), purity (*śauca),* forbearance (*kṣānti*) uprightness (*ārjava*), wisdom (*Jñāna*), knowledge (*vijñāna*) faith in religion (*āstikya*).[9]
   - (b) Duties—studying and teaching of the Vedas, performance of sacrifices (*yajña*), giving and accepting alms.[10]
2. *Qualities and duties of a Kṣatriya:*
   - (a) Qualities: heroism (*śaurya*), vigour (*teja*), steadiness (*dhṛti*), resourcefulness (*dākṣya*), not fleeing from a battle, generosity and leadership (*īśvarabhāva*).[11]
   - (b) *Duties:* Protecting people from external aggression and internal disturbances as well as governing them with a view to

peace and prosperity, chastising the wicked (*asādhunigraha*), charity (*dāna*).

3. *Duties of a Vaiśya*: agriculture, tending cattle and trade.[12]
4. *Duties of Śūdra*: service to the other three classes.[13]

B. ***Āśrama Dharma* (mainly based on *Padārthadharmasaṅgraha* of Praśastapāda—Tr. G.N. Jha):**

1. *Duties/Qualities of a Brahmacārī*—Attendance upon the teacher, fetching of fuel, offering incense to the sacrificial fire, living on alms in the manner prescribed by the scriptures, avoidance of such things as wine, meat, sleeping during day time, painting of the eyes etc.
   In short, the duty of a *Brahmacārī* is to lead a celibate life based on simplicity, chastity, austerity and obedience.
2. *Duties of a Gṛhaṣtha*—(a) The morning and evening offering of the five great sacrifices—*bhūtayajña* (sacrifice to animals), *manuṣyayajña* (sacrifice to men in the form of serving and entertaining of guests— *atithi pujanam manuṣya yajñaḥ*) *devayajña* (sacrifice to gods in the form of offering incense to the sacred fire—*homaḥ devayajñaḥ*), *pitṛyajña* (sacrifice to ancestors in the form of paying respect to them by observing *śrāddha* rites *śrāddham pitṛyajñaḥ*), and *Brahmayajña* (sacrifice to *Brahma* or the Veda by reading sacred texts—*Vedapāṭhaḥ Brahmayajñaḥ*), (b) The taking of the *Ekāgni* Fire and the offering into it the absolutely necessary *Pākayajña* sacrifices and also, if possible, of such sacrifices as those of *Agnādhyeya*, the *Haviryajña*, the *Agnistoma* and the *Somayajñas.* (c) Begetting of children, but abstaining from sexual intercourse at improper times.
3. *Duties of a Vānaprastha*—Living in a forest, wearing skin and bark of trees, non-shaving of hair and beard and non-cutting of nails, living only on fruits of the jungle and those also as are left after the sacrifices.

Manu, however, givs a more detailed account of the qualities and duties of a *vānaprastha* with moral significance. Besides the above, he says the *vānaprastha* should continue to offer the five great sacrifices like the householder, the only difference being that whereas the householder performs the sacrifices with the aim of attaining *artha* and *kāma*, the *vānaprastha* is inspired by no such worldly motive. Inspired by the Vedas, he has always to be active in reciting the Vedas, and has to be prompted in *dharma* by exercising such moral qualities as forbearance, friendship, liberality; peace of mind, wisdom and compassion towards all creatures.[14]

4. *Qualities/Duties of a Sannyāsin*—A *sannyāsin* is a wandering ascetic, completely devoid of all sorts of passions and desires. No specific duties are prescribed for him. He is, in a sense, a supra-ethical being. But still he is expected not to neglect the internal and external duties as envisaged in the forms of *yamas* and *niyamas*. Such a man is known by the serenity of his mind, his gentleness, his compassion for all creatures and a complete annihilation on his part of the fire of passions. He is completely indifferent to worldly gains and is firm in his meditation and concentration upon *Brhaman*. Regarding the specific qualities or characteristics of a *sannyāsin*, Manu says: He puts down his feet on a soil which looks pure by his very sight, he drinks water pruified by a cloth, he utters words purified by truth and performs acts as purified by his mind (or as deemed pure by his mind). He bears harsh words patiently, he does not insult anybody and he does not become anybody's enemy for the sake of his perishable body. He does not show anger to an angry man in return, he blesses even those who curse him, and he does not utter gossip (or speech devoid of significance and truth) emanating from the seven gates (meaning thereby, perhaps, the five sense-organs, mind and intellect).[15]

4. Buddhism and Jainism

We have so far drawn out elaborate lists of virtues and duties we find in the various systems of Indian tradition. But, specifically speaking, they are virtues and duties mentioned in the Hindu tradition only. Indian tradition includes, besids others, Jaina and Bauddha traditions also, which despite many similarities with Hinduism, have their own specialities. We shall have therefore to see in brief a record of virtues and duties recognised in these two important traditions also.

As a matter of fact, we have already noted the essential Buddhist and Jaina virtues in our Chapter VI. We have seen that the essential Buddhist virtues consist in what is called the *Pañcaśīla* and the Jaina virtues in *Pañcamahāvrata*. Both are essentially the same as the five *yamas* of Hindu tradition. However, the *Pañcaśīla* of Buddhism is interpreted and understood in a more positive manner so that virtues (or duties) under it seem more socially oriented in implication an application. At least the Western thinkers take Buddhist list of virtues more socially oriented than the Hindu one. I, for myself, am not disposed to make any clear distinction beteween Hinduism and Buddhism on this count. To me it seems, as I have also indicated in the sixth chapter, that all the three religions of Indian tradition lay greater emphasis on virtues of individual purity than on the social virtues, without however ignoring the latter's importance. This is, as a matter of fact, involved in the Indian concept of morality itself, as we have seen in our first chapter. If we go through the *aṭṭha* and *dasa śīlas* of Buddhism and various *anuvratas* of Jainism, we shall find that these two religions are rather more keen on emphasizing ascetic and monkist virtues of self-purity, self-discipline and self-concentration than what Hinduism does on that front. It is, of course, a fact that by rejecting Vedic ceremonialism and ritualism, both Buddhism and Jainism become able to give their virtues of individual purity rather a more ethical touch than Hinduism could do. The virtues (as well as duties), however, emphasized in all the three traditions are, more or less, the same, if we limit our consideration of virtues to what has been called *sāmānya dharmas* in the Hindu tradition. The Buddhist and Jaina traditions, as a matter of fact, do not have any scope for what is known as *varṇāśrama dharmas.* These *dharmas* are peculiar to Hinduism alone. Buddhism and jainism prescribe qualities of character and conduct which are equally applicable to all. They make a distinction between the duties of an ordinary man and those of a monk, the latter's duties being more rigorous and ascetic.

5. A General Estimate

On the whole, it can be said about the Indian lists of virtues and duties that by going through them one can hardly miss being impressed by their subtlety and depth. The Indian thinkers are to be admired for their vision of human qualities of character. They count both virtues and vices in great details and count them so minutely that hardly any quality worth considering is left out. Sometimes they are so elaborate that they distinguish between qualities related to body, speech and mind separately. Giving a separate status to qualities (good and bad both) relating to speech is a special characteristic of the Indian moral thinkers. In the West, perhaps, no virtue related to speech, other than veracious speech, has been recognised.

The Hindu distinction between the *sādhāraṇa* and *varṇāśrama dharmas* has also its speciality and significance. *Sādhāraṇa dharmas* are for all alike. Everyone, irrespective of the class or status, has to observe these *dharmas.* Certain *dharmas* become obligatory for one by virtue of his being the member of a particular class or his passing through a particular stage of life. The class division has the inherent recognition of the natural fact that men cannot be equally fit and efficient for all kinds of social duties. Social duties demand what may be called division of labour. The different phases of life is based on the apparent realisation of the fact that life is a staircase on which one can ascend gradually by way of discharging necessary duties relative to each stage. For ascending higher and higher in the scale of life, it is necessary to divide it into certain broad phases.

It may be pointed out here that the greatest evil of the Hindu scheme of *dharmas* is the degradation of the *śūdras* in the society. But it seems to me that if the things are taken in the right perspective, there is no cause for degrading the *śūdras* to an extent to which some of the Smṛtikāras seem to have done. At least the distinction of *dharmas* into *sādhāraṇa* and *varṇāśrama* has nothing in its spirit which may serve as a real cause for denigrading the *śūdras*. The *varṇa dharma* itself is based not only on the concept of division of labour, but also on the concept of dignity of labour. The services of all classes have been deemed to be equally valuable for the society in their own ways. Moreover, as specially in the *Bhagavadgītā* the emphasis on the observance of *svadharma*, i.e. one's own *dharma* in accordance with one's *varṇa* and *āśrama*, for reaching one's highest destiny amply demonstrates the equal worth and value of the services of all classes.

The recognition of the *sādhāraṇa dharmas* as somewhat supervening upon the *varṇāśrama dharmas* also aims at giving to all persons, including the *śūdras*, equality of status. The *sādhāraṇa dharmas* are as much meant for, or in relation to, *śūdras* as for, or in relation to, others. These *dharmas* are to be used in respect of the *śūdras* in the same manner and in the same spirit in which they are to be used in respect of the members of other *varṇas*. Thus, so far as the *sādhāraṇa dharmas* are concerned, the *śūdras* are given the same status as others. By way of contrasting the status of a barbarian in the platonic scheme of social classification, Maitra remarks very aptly in this connection: "For Plato the barbarian is without any moral standing there are not only no duties to be fulfilled by him but also no duties to be fulfilled in respect of him. The Hindu, however, in spite of the social degradation of the *śūdra* does not exclude him altogether from moral protection, but shelters him from persecution through a code of universal duties which are obligatory on man as man. These duties are to be observed by all alike, being the duties obligatory in his dealings with everybody else."[16]

We have hinted above that of the two kinds of *dharmas—sādhāraṇa* and *varṇāśrama*—the former has been accorded a superior status. But the matter does not seem to be so straight-forward and clear-cut when we go through some actual instances of conflict in the Hindu tradition. In the *Rāmāyaṇa,* for example, instances can be found in which *sādhāraṇa dharmas* seem to have superseded the *varṇāśrama dharmas*, but in the *Mahābhārata* it is not so. Rāma, while giving lessons of *dharma* to the angry Lakṣamaṇa on the occasion of the former's preparing for the jungle on the order of his father, points out to the latter that here in this case in place of following his *kṣātra dharma* (of fighting with or killing anyone who comes in the way of Rāma's enthronement), Lakṣamaṇa should follow the *sādhāraṇa dharma* of obeying the parents. Because, according to him, the *kṣātra dharma (varṇa dharma)* was lower in status than the *sādhāraṇa dharma.* But in he *Mahābhārata* it may be seen that Kṛṣṇa induces Arjuna to fight of the strong plea that observing one's *svadharma* (another name for *varṇāśrama dharma*) was one's foremost duty. *Ahiṃsā* is widely recognised as *sādhāraṇa dharma* in the Hindu tradition, but Kṛṣṇa advises Arjuna to resort to *hiṃsā* for the sake of *svadharma.* That way the *sādhāraṇa dharma* is placed at a lower pedestal than the *varṇa dharma,* although in general spirit the *sādhāraṇa dharmas* seem to supervene over the *varnāśrama dharmas.* But in any case in the Hindu tradition the supreme importance and value of the distinction between *sādhāraṇa* and *varṇāśrama dharmas* in human life cannot be ignored.

REFERENCES

1. Leslie Stephen, *The Science of Ethics* (New York: G.P. Putnam's Sons, 1882), p. 155.
2. William Frankena, *Ethics*, p. 65.
3. S.K. Maitra, *op. cit.*, p. 8.
4. For example, in X.63 and XII.83 Manu has counted *Ahiṃsā* as a virtue.
5. *Āpastamba*, 1.8.13.5.
6. *Ibid.*, 1.8.14.6.
7. *BG* XVI.1-3.
8. S.K. Maitra, *op. cit.*, p. 209.
9. *BG* XVIII.43.
10. *Manu* 1.88.
11. *BG* XVIII.43.
12. *BG* VIII.44.

13. *Ibid.*
14. *Manu* VI.8.
15. *Manu* VI.46-48.
16. S.K. Maitra, *op. cit.*, p. 17.

CHAPTER IX

Dharma and Mokṣa

With the exception of the Cārvāka, which is the lone materialistic system in the Indian philosophical tradition, almost all the Indian systems recognise *Mokṣa* to be the highest good of life. It has, of course, sometimes been named as *Nirvāṇa, Kaivalya, Apavarga* etc. also. Generally speaking, *Mokṣa* is a non-moral value symbolising a status free from all worldly limitations. It is freedom from subjection to time, from birth and death, and thus from all consequent suffering of worldly existence. These are some general points about the nature of *Mokṣa* to which all the Indian systems agree, but they differ significantly about other dertails of its nature. A brief survey of the concept of *Mokṣa* with reference to the Indian systems may pave the way for a fuller idea as to what is understood to be the highest good of life in the Indian tradition.

1. The Concept of *Mokṣa*

(a) *The Vedas, the Upaniṣads and the Bhagavadgītā*

In the Vedas, idea about *Mokṣa* is hardly clear. Heaven, a place of eternal pleasure and rejoice, is the highest good of life. It is in the Upaniṣads that we first get an idea about *Mokṣa*. Here sometimes *Mokṣa* is understood as an identity of self with the *Brahman*, the ultimate reality, and sometimes as likeness of the self with God. The *Bṛhadāraṇyaka Upaniṣad* describes the state of *Mokṣa* thus: "As a man in the embrace of his beloved wife knows nothing without or within, so the person when in the embrace of the Intelligent self knows nothing without or within. That, verily, is his form in which his desire is fulfilled, in which the self is his desire, in which he is without desire, free from any sorrow."[1] Gaudapāda in his Kārikā on *Māṇḍūkya Up.* gives an account of *Mokṣa* which is more thoroughly a state of absorption into the universal nature of *Brahman:* "As on the destruction of the jar etc. the ether enclosed in the jar etc. merges with the *ākāśa,* even so the individual merges into the universal spirit."[2] But the *Maṇḍukya* itself says at another place that by liberation the soul attains likeness with the Divine.[3] It is due to these two trends present in the Upaniṣads that Śaṃkara and Rāmānuja interpret *Mokṣa* differently, the former as identity of self with *Brahman* and the latter as communion with God. The *Gītā* also seems to emphasize equivalence (*sādharmya*) with God as the nature of *Mokṣa*, and not identity with God. However, the *Gītā* describes *Mokṣa* variously at various places —as emnacipation, as eternal state, as the highest rest, as the entering into God, as contact with God, as rest in *Brahman*, as transformation into the Divine existence, as transmutation into Godhead and so on.

(b) *The Nyāya-Vaiśeṣika*

The systems also differ amongst themselves as to the detailed nature of *Mokṣa*. The Nyāya-Vaiśeṣika takes it as a purely negative state in which the soul becomes completely free from all the *kleṣas* (*rāga, dveṣa* and *moha*), from all the merits and demerits, from the continuous cycle of birth and death, from all experience of pleasure and pain and, as a matter of fact, from all consciousness too. Consciousness is not the inherent quality of soul according to the Nyāya-Vaiśeṣika. It is brought into it through its contact with the mind and the sense-organs. And as such a contact is absent in the state of *Mokṣa*, so the soul in this state has absolutely no experience, no consciousness. In liberation no positive bliss is attained. Only there is a complete cessation of all sufferings. "Release is the absolute deliverance from pain," says the *Nyāya-Sūtra* (*tadatyanta vimokṣaḥ apavargaḥ*).[4] Hence, nothing positive is attained in the state of liberation. It is a state of pure negation, of the negation of all sufferings.

(c) *The Sāṃkhya*

According to the Sāṃkhya also, *Mokṣa* is complete freedom from all sufferings. Sāṃkhya recognises three kinds of suffering (*trividha duḥkha*) and it is complete freedom from these three kinds of suffering that is called *Mokṣa* (*trividha duḥkhātyanta-nivṛttiratyanta-puruṣārthaḥ*).[5] Unlike the Nyāya-Vaiśeṣika, however, the Sāṃkhya takes consciousness as the very essence of soul and therefore by attaining *Mokṣa* the soul attains its pure conscious nature. It thus regains its inherent nature which it had, in a way, lost due to its identifying itself with *prakṛti* as a result of ignorance. The moment the discriminative knowledge dawns upon the soul, it regains its original nature of pure consciousness. In this state there is neither pleasure nor pain, because pleasure and pain are the modes of *prakṛti*. *Puruṣa* or self in its pure nature is completely above these mundance modes.

(d) ***The Mīmāṃsā***

The Mīmāṃsā conception of *Mokṣa* is a bit ambiguous and imprecise. Opinions therefore differ as to the exact nature of *Mokṣa* as understood and depicted in the Mīmāṃsā. According to one view, the Mīmāṃsā like the Nyāya-Vaiśeṣika professes a purely negative view of *Mokṣa* in which the soul after attaining liberation simply gets rid of its accumulated merit-demerit, pleasure-pain etc. Attainment of *Mokṣa* is not attaining any state of bliss, for, if liberation consists in the experience of bliss, then it will be of the nature of heaven which is something transient, and not eternal. But liberation is something eternal, and therefore it cannot be of the nature of pleasure or bliss.

The above view of *Mokṣa* is often attributed to the Kumārila school of Mīmāṃsā. Such a view is expressed by Pārthasārathi Mishra in his *Śāstradīpikā*. Explaining the point further, he says that with liberation the soul is restored to its primitive condition. In other words, the freed soul abides in itself. Clarifying what 'abiding in itself' means, Pārthasārathi Mishra points out that it is the natural state in which the soul's own potency to cognise, existence, substanceness etc. persist.[6] Because mind is absent in the state of liberation, the feeling of pleasure is also absent.

There are others such as Anantadeo who maintain that Kumārila believes *Mokṣa* to be a positive state of bliss. As a matter of fact, there seems to be discrepancy between Kumārila's own works *Ślokavārtika* and *Tantravārtika* on this point. The former seems to depict a negative view of *Mokṣa*, while the latter a positive view.

About Prabhākara it is said that he also, more or less, falls in line with Kumārila in his conception of *Mokṣa*. He takes *Mokṣa* as the final riddance form future births brought in by the extinction of both *dharma* and *adharma*.[7] However, Dr. Ganganath Jha makes the following remark regarding Prahbākara's view on *Mokṣa:* "The view of Prabhākara himself we have no direct means of ascertaining as, like Sabara, he does not deal with people who have transcended *Karma* or Action. His followers' views on the subject we have from the *Prakaraṇapañcikā*. According to these views liberation consists in the disappearance of all Merits and Demerits accruing to the Soul that it is born in the physical body; consequently when all Merits and Demerits have disappeared, there remains nothing that could lead the Soul to be born again in the body; and the Soul ceases to have connection with the body and hence also with the sense-organs etc., all its metempsychic troubles are ended and it is free, liberated."[8] From the remark it seems obvious that Prabhākara also has a merely negative conception of *Mokṣa*.

(e) *The Vedānta (Śaṃkara and Rāmānuja)*

Śaṃkara and Rāmānuja take a positive view of *Mokṣa*. That is, according to them, *Mokṣa* is not only getting rid of the cycle of life and death and consequently of all sufferings, but also attainment of a positive state of bliss. The soul in the liberated state attains its true nature which is pure consciousness and bliss. However, despite this general agreement, Śaṃkara and Rāmānuja differ significantly between themselves regarding the nature of *Mokṣa*. This difference is mainly due to their differences in view regarding the nature of soul itself in relation to *Brahman*, the ultimate reality.

According to Śaṃkara, the soul in its true nature is identical with *Brahman*, while according to Rāmānuja, the former is only a part or a mode of *Brahman*. According to both of them liberation means the realisation by the soul of its true nature. According to Śaṃkara, this realisation consists in soul's experience of its identity with *Brahman*, while Rāmānuja holds it is the realisation by the soul of its being a real mode or expression of *Brahman*. According to Śaṃkara, the soul becomes *Brahman* in liberation, but according to Rāmānuja it only becomes like *Brhman*. Moreover, whereas according to Śaṁkara, the soul after liberation loses its separate identity, according to Rāmānuja, the soul maintains separate identity even after liberation, because it becomes only similar to *Brahman*, and not *Brahman* himself. In any case however, according to both these thinkers, the soul not only gets rid of certain things in liberation, rather it also achieves the positive state of pure knowledge and eternal bliss.

(f) *Buddhism*

Of the two non-orthodox schools of Indian thought which believe in *Mokṣa* as the ultimate destiny, Buddhism is generally recognised as having a negative concept of *Mokṣa* (although the point is controversial) while Jainism a fairly positive one. Buddhism terms liberation as *Nirvāṇa* which literally means 'cooling down' or 'blowing out'. The meaning itself shows that *Nirvāṇa* is basically a negative concept. The blowing out (or cooling down) means here the blowing out (or cooling down) of the fire of passions. It is well-known that according to Buddhism it is the passions which are the root cause of bondage or suffering. So when the passions are blown out, liberation is attained. With the cooling down of passions, actions cease bearing fruits and consequently the cycle of birth and death stops. And that is really the complete cessation of suffering, which is the true nature of *Nirvāṇa*. But according to some, *Nirvāṇa* is not merely a negative state. They point out that when the fire of passions cools down, it is quite natural that a state of perfect peace and equanimity will be achieved and this is a positive achievement. Not only that, some quite unambiguously believe that *Nirvāṇa* brings positive bliss. "*nibbānam paramam sukham*"[9], says the *Dhammapada*. This state of happiness is unique, which cannot be described in words.

(g) *Jainism*

The Jaina conception of *Mokṣa* is positive consequence of the Jaina conception of soul. Jainism believes that the soul in its inherent nature possesses four infinites (*ananta catuṣṭaya*)—infinite bliss, infinite power, infinite faith and infinite knowledge. It is only due to its association with the matter that the soul loses its inherent nature and falls in bondage. So, naturally by attaining *Mokṣa*, the soul is not only free from the chain of birth and rebirth and from consequent suffering, but it also attains its inherent nature consisting of the above four infinites.

(h) *General Remarks*

We have made a passing survey of the various concepts of *Mokṣa* present in the Indian tradition. Differences notwithstanding, there is an essential agreement about the negative attainment of the state of *Mokṣa*. All the systems agree at least in the fact that *Mokṣa* is complete riddance from all sufferings, from the cycle of birth and death and from all sorts of passions and desires. In one sense, there is a general agreement on some positive attainment also. Every system admits in its own way that by attaining liberation, the soul attains its original inherent nature. Thus in a sense according to all the systems, *Mokṣa* is *ātma svarupa lābha*. The *Bhāgvata* seemingly represents the spirit of the whole of Indian tradition when it describes *Mokṣa* as the attainment of individual's natural state by relinquishing its imposed state (*muktir hitvānyathārūpam, svarūpeṇa vyavasthitiḥ*). Radhakrishnan also seems to share the same view when he says after considering the various conceptions of *Mokṣa*, "All views agree that eternal life is an absolute fulfilment of what we are, the final affirmation of our progressive self-finding."[10]

Again, *Mokṣa* as the highest ideal of life is a non-moral or rather a supra-moral state, about which no judgement of rightness or wrongness, goodness or badness is to be passed. By attaining this man becomes completely free from all bonds of empirical life, including the moral bond. He rises above the fetters of duty and obligation. This, however, means neither that the liberated man is necessarily to take to inaction nor that he is free to do even immoral acts. The point assumes real significance in face of the concept of *Jīvan-mukti*. Systems like Sāṃkhya, Advaita Vedānta and Buddhism believe in this kind of *Mukti*. As the name indicates, *Jīvan-mukti* means attaining *Mokṣa* in this very life. According to this view, annihilation of physical body is not necessary for liberation. What is necessary is the removal of passions and ignorance. For Sāṃkhya the moment one has the discriminative knowledge of the duality of *puruṣa* and *prakṛti* he is liberated. Similarly, according to Advaita Vedānta, the moment one attains the knowledge of the identity between the self and *Brahman*, he is liberated. For liberation the end of the present life is not necessary. According to Buddhism, again, *Nirvāṇa* is not the cessation of physical life, it is the cessation of passions (*tṛṣṇā*) alone. So the moment one becomes free from the fire of *tṛṣṇā*, he is liberated. The question of action, duty or obligation arises in the case of such liberated persons alone. Those who attain *Videha mukti*, i.e. *Mokṣa* after the end of physical life, question of activity does not at all arise. It is thus for the *Jīva muktas* that it is said that even in spite of rising above the fetters of duty and obligation, they are not necessarily to take to inaction nor do they get license to do even immoral acts. Their being free from any moral binding simply means that they now attain such an unstained status free from all egoistic passions and *doṣas* that it is impossible for them to perform evil actions. It now becomes their nature to perform actions for the good of others. Righteousness now necessarily follows from their very nature. As the ego of such men completely burns out, they become completely *niṣkāma*. So only *niṣkāma karmas* follow out of their nature.

2. The Role of *Dharma* in *Mokṣa*

The concept of *Mokṣa* with reference to the different Indian systems thus stated, let us now see what role *dharma* has to play in leading us to our ultimate goal of *Mokṣa*. Generally speaking, it may be said that because bondage is the result of ignorance, so liberation will result out of knowledge. Therefore *dharma* perhaps cannot have any role in leading us to the path of liberation. Moreover, *dharma* consists of virtues and duties which involve actions. Actions, right or wrong, bind. So, how can *dharma* be a means to liberation? Perhaps it is due to this fact that hardly any Indian system believes that *dharma* directly (or by itself) leads to *Mokṣa*. But then this does not mean that *dharma* has no role or that it has only a very insignificant and negligible role in getting us liberated. *Dharma* has its role and in some systems it has a major role too. Let us see the position in each system:

(a) ***The Vedas and the Upaniṣads***

In the Vedas we find the works—the ritualistic practices—as means to our highest goal. But the Vedas hardly contain any idea of *Mokṣa* as the highest goal. Heaven, a place of abiding pleasure and rejoice, is taken as the highest goal that is attainable by pleasing gods through ritualistic practices. Whether ritualistic acts can be taken as constituting part of *dharma* itself may be controversial. We may see that ritualistic acts have their place in *dharma* even in systems beyond the Vedas. For example, within the scheme of *varṇāśrama dharmas* there is scope for rituals and these *dharmas* have their important place in almost all the Indian systems. Within the *nityanaimittika karmas* of the Mīmāṃsakas, again, rituals have got an important place, and the performance of these *karmas* is an esssential part of one's *dharma*, according to the Mīmāṃsakas. So *dharma*, as it is seen to be understood in the Indian tradition, seems to include at least certain important rituals within it. If, however, *dharma* is taken as designating pure morality in the sense of generally recognised moral virtues and duties as distinguished from religious duties, the case of rituals as forming constituents of *dharma* may then be weaker. But elements of pure morality are also not completely absent in the Vedas. We have seen that the Vedas have various good qualities and acts (virtues and duties). It is, however, not clear how far the inculcation of these qualities and the performance of purely moral acts add potentially or significantly to the attainment of the highest goal. From a general understanding of the Vedas rituals appear to have a superior role in that direction.

It is in the Upaniṣads, we have seen, that *Mokṣa* for the first time has been taken as the highest goal of man. This goal is attainable primarily by knowledge according to the Upaniṣads—the knowledge of *Ātman* or *Brahman*. But then we have seen that for the attainment of this knowledge, practising of virtue is also necessary according to the Upaniṣads. A man devoid of virtuous conduct can hardly be able to attain knowledge. The *Kaṭha Upaniṣad* is very clear in this regard when it asserts that he who has not ceased from evil conduct cannot obtain Him by knowledge alone (11.24). So, although *Mokṣa* is finally a result of *jñāna*, moral effort is also necessary for it. About the attitude of the Upaniṣads regarding the relative significance of knowledge and morality in our effort to attain *Mokṣa*, Hopkins very significantly remarks "There was no such superficial distinction as is made with us between 'education' and 'character' as the goal of learning and life. Education implied character, there was no knowledge without its ethical counterpart."[11]

(b) *The Bhagavadgītā*

The *Bhagavadgītā* is generally taken as depicting three alternative paths, each equally effective, for the attainment of *Mokṣa*. These are: the path of knowledge, the path of devotion and the path of action (the path of *dharma* or morality). This is also generally recognised that these three are independent paths in the sense that one can attain liberation taking recourse to anyone of them. In yet another sense the paths are mutually interdependent so much so that a faithful pursuit of anyone of them will automatically lead to following the other two. We are not, however, going here into the details of all these propositions.

We are simply concerned here with the role that the *Bhagavadgītā* assigns to *dharma* in our realisation of *Mokṣa*. The *Bhagavadgītā* assigns the path of action an equal status with that of knowledge or devotion in the attainment of *Mokṣa*. So, *dharma* is assigned the full status. For *dharma* consists mainly in the performance of various duties—sacrificial or morally virtuous. In the main, *Gītā* emphasizes non-attached actions to be the essential consitituent of the path of action. In other words, the path of action mainly consists, according to the *Gītā*, of the non-attached actions, i.e. actions done with no egoistic end in view. However, *varṇāśrama dharmas* have been given very respectable place in the *Gītā*. Designated mainly as *svadharma*, they have been regarded as the sure and essential means to liberation. It is said that if anybody fulfils his *svadharma* quite faithfully without taking recourse to the *svadharma* of any other, he is sure to get liberation. While counselling Arjuna to fight the *Mahābhārata* battle, Kṛṣṇa was always emphasizing before Arjuna the importance of following one's *svadharma* for getting final liberation. However, in the path of action, the lesson of *niṣkāma karma* is supreme in the *Gītā*. Even one's *svadharma* is to be followed in a non-attached manner. Besides *varṇāśrama dharmas* there are a lot of *sādhāraṇa dharmas* also enumerated in the *Bhagavadgītā* (which we have seen earlier) whose observance is deemed necessary as a path to liberation. So, in all these ways, *dharma* has been accorded an important place in the *Gītā* as a path to liberation.

(c) *The Nyāya-Vaiśeṣika*

When we come to the systems, we find that the Nyāya-Vaiśeṣika, like many other systems, takes knowledge to be the ultimate source of *Mokṣa*. But then performance of *dharma* also is deemed necessary for that. As a matter of fact, the Nyāya-Vaiśeṣika presents a doctrine of *Mokṣa-sādhana* which is known as *samuccayavāda*. According to it *Mokṣa* is a result of a joint effort made in the form of the observance of *dharma* and the pursuit of knolwedge. The Nyāya-Vaiśeṣika points out that it is a fact that actions bind, but not all actions do so. Only such actions bind which are done with egoistic motives. Such actions which are our unconditional duties (*dharmas*) do not bind. The necessary obligatory duties (*nitya karmas*) and the duties prescribed by our Śāstras for special occasions (*naimittika karmas*) do not bind. As a matter of fact, the performance of such *dharmas* is not optional, it is compulsory for a seeker of *Mokṣa* to perform them.

It is said in the *Padārthadharmasaṃgraha* of Praśastapāda that not only it is that the non-performance of these *dharmas* delays *Mokṣa*, rather their non-performance has a tendency to bind. The non-performance of duties, it is said, is a negative fact which can not produce any positive binding effect. Praśastapāda replies that the non-performance of prescribed *dharmas* allows occasions in which sin is produced by other causes set in motion and it is this sin which has a binding effect. So the performance of *dharma* in the form of the *nityanaimittika karmas* is necessary according to the Nyāya-Vaiśeṣika for the attainment of *Mokṣa*. Not only that, an honest and faithful observance of the various acts under *sādhāraṇa dharmas* as well as the observance of the *varṇāśrama dharmas* leads a long way towards the attainment of liberation.

(d) ***The Sāṃkhya***

Apparently, the Sāṃkhya seems to insist on mere knowledge as the path to liberation, giving no place to the performance of *dharmas* in this connection. According to it, liberation means discriminatory knowledge, i.e., the knowledge of absolute discrimination between *Puruṣa* and *Prakṛti*. Works or actions cannot have any place in leading us to such a state of *Mokṣa*, because no amount of action done can produce the knowledge in us required for *Mokṣa*. So only the path of knowledge can lead us to the goal. It does not require work either as an alternative means or as a cooperative assistant. (*niyatakāraṇatvānna samuccaya vikalpau*).[12] Works of any kind, whether conditional or unconditional (*kāmya* or *akāmya*) are simply irrelevant in this connection (*kāmye'kāmye'pi sādhyatvāviśeṣāt*).[13] Liberation is to come from knowledge alone. By works one can attain heaven, but that is only temporary relief form pain, not *Mokṣa*.

It appears on the basis of the above that for Sāṃkhya there is absolutely no place of *dharma* in the attainment of *Mokṣa;* only knowledge can lead us to *Mokṣa*. But we must be careful here about the use of actual words and their real meaning. Sāṃkhya declares the uselessness of 'works' (*karma*) in the attainment of *Mokṣa* and not of '*dharma*' in all its implications and applications. As a matter of fact, when Sāṃkhya advises us to desist from works or actions, it simply asks us to desist from the sacrificial and ritualistic acts of the Vedas. But these actions clearly do not constitute the whole of *dharma*. Acts of self-discipline and self-purification as well as those which have social implications constitute *dharma*. Sāṃkhya has full appreciation for acts of self-discipline. In fact, such acts are necessary for leading us to *jñāna*. Here we shall make good of our point if we make a distinction between knowledge as path (*jñāna mārga*) and knowledge as end: (*jñāna*). According to Sāṃkhya, knowledge itself is the end, the knowledge of absolute distinction between *Puruṣa* and *Prakṛti*. So when Sāṃkhya says that *Mokṣa* is to be attainable only by knowledge, not by acts, it certainly speaks of knowledge as a path and not of knowledge as end. The former must consist in some process, in certain steps which ultimately lead to knowledge as end, i.e., *Mokṣa*. So, what is this knowledge as a path? According to Sāṃkhya, this path consists in removing the obstacles which lie in the path of knowledge as liberation. These obstacles are the various passions, and control of senses and mind is necessary for removing them. For that again what is necessary is meditation. Passions are removed by meditation (*rāgopahatirdhyānam*).[14]

The practices conducive to meditation are: restraint, postures and one's duties. Restraint means restraint of breath. Postures mean the various bodily postures as envisaged by the Yoga system of Patañjali. And one's duties means duties relating to one's *āśrama*. (*svakarma svāśrama vihita karmānuṣṭhānam*).[15] So, Sāṃkhya believes in the performance of various acts of self-discipline including the *āśrama dharmas* as conducive to *Mokṣa*. They form in a sense part of the *jñāna-mārga* itself. Moreover, Sāṃkhya is not averse even to the performance of certain virtuous social duties. It believes in the distinction between good and bad actions and also believes that the former lead one nearer to the goal of *Mokṣa*. In accordance with its belief in the reality of the three *guṇas* Sāṃkhya makes a distinction between three kinds of acts which may be regarded as ethically significant: (1) *Sāttvika* actions which consist in kindness, restraint of sense-organs, freedom from hatred etc. (2) *Rājasika* actions such as anger, greed, violence etc. (3) *Tāmasika* actions such as lust, intoxication etc. Sāṃkhya highly recommends the performance of the first kind of actions while desisting from the other two. Furthermore, it has a general sympathy with the *aṣṭāṅgika yoga-mārga* of Patañjali, which includes within it the *yamas* end *niyamas*. These *yamas* and *niyamas,* we have seen, include virtues (as well as duties) pertaining to both individual and social morality. So, taking into consideration all these facts, it cannot be said that Sāṃkhya is totally averse to the role of *dharma* (or morality) in the attainment of liberation

(e) *The Mīmāṃsā*

The Mīmāṃsakas seem to recognise the roles of both *karma* and *jñāna* in the attainment of *Mokṣa,* but they decidedly lay greater emphasis upon the former. By *karma,* they mean the essential or unconditional *karmas* as prescribed by the Vedas. Such *karmas* they call *nityanaimittika karmas* and characterise them as *dharma* proper. It is well-known that the Mīmāṃsakas define *dharma* in terms of Vedic injunctions and of such injunctions those which prompt what is called the *nityanaimittika karmas* are the most prominent. *Karmas* are of three kinds according to the Mīmāṃsakas: (1) *kāmya* (interested or attached), (2) *Nisiddha* (prohibited), and (3) *Nityanaimittika* (unconditional or necessarily obligatory). The performance of the first two kinds of *karmas* further bind. The third kind of *karmas* do not hind, rather they have a liberating effect. Their performance removes the *sañcita karmas* which are the proximate cause of bondage. It is such actions which accumulate the potency of *Apūrva.* For *Mokṣa* it is necessary to annihilate the potency. This is possible, according to the Mīmāṃsakas, only by the performance of unconditional duties. Knowledge, of course, has its role in our attainment of *Mokṣa,* because what keeps us in bondage is our ignorance. Knowledge by itself is not capable of removing the immediate proximate cause of bondage, i.e., the accumulated potency of past actions. For that the performance of unconditional duties is necessary. The non-performance of these actions does not only debar one from achieving good results, rather he will thereby be committing positive sin to further delay the chances of deliverence. Kumārila clearly says in his *Ślokavārtika:* "One desiring deliverence, therefore, would not engage in such actions as are either prohibited or enjoined with a view to attaining certain (material) results. But he would continue to perform those that are enjoined as necessary (to be performed daily) and those that are enjoined to be performed on certain occasions (such as eclipses and the like) in order to avoid sin (accruing for the non-performance of such duties)."[16]

About the inefficacy of mere knowledge as the means to liberation, Kumārila says again, "Though it is understood that actions are like attachment etc. brought about by ignorance, yet knowledge cannot set aside those actions as existing in a state of latent potentiality. That there is destruction of actions by knowledge is not proved. That 'self is to be known' has not been enjoined with a view to the attainment of deliverence. All that it indicates is the fact that knowledge of self is a cause of activity towards certain sacrifices."[17] Thus knowledge, according to Kumārila, is not the direct cause of liberation. It only helps in the discharge of proper duties. The direct cause of our liberation is the performance of our essential *dharmas*, the essential or unconditional duties. Kumārila actually criticises the Sāṃkhya doctrine which assumes mere knowledge to be the cause of liberation. Kumārila therefore preaches, as Pārtharsārathi Mishra says in his *Śāstradīpikā*, a kind of *samuccayavāda.*[18] But it is clear from the above that the *samuccaya* does not give equal importance to both *jñāna* and *karma*. The latter is definitely given greater importance. So, Mīmāṃsā is one system which in terms of its own understanding of *dharma* gives it utmost importance as a means to liberation.

Prabhākara also seems to hold more or less a similar view in this regard. He asserts that *Mokṣa* is to be attained by the performance of *nitya-naimittika karmas* in association with *Ātma-jñāna*. Knowledge of the self is no doubt necessary for both *karma* and *Mokṣa*, for *kṛtavartha* and *puruṣārtha*, but *Mokṣa* is directly the result of the performance of the unconditional duties. Such a view seems to be put forth in the *Prakaraṇapañcikā* (p. 156) where it is said that all prior mertis and demerits and the further accumulation of them are done away with by ceasing to perform *pratisiddha karmas*, by performing the *nitya karmas* and by the knowledge of the soul aided by such virtues as contentment, self-control etc.[19] So, here besides the performance of sacrificial duties, there is also a mention of finer ethical virtues like contentment and self-control as leading to *Mokṣa*.

(f) *The Śaṃkara Vedānta*

Like Sāṃkhya, Śaṃkara also believes that knowledge alone is capable of giving us *Mokṣa;* performance of *dhārmika* activities is not at all necessary for that. *Mokṣa* is knowledge of the identity between self and *Brahman* and this knowledge as end is attainable only by knowledge as means. Śaṃkara openly speaks against the efficacy of works as leading to *Mokṣa*. He points out that if *Mokṣa* were the product of works, then it will be something non-eternal because the fruit of actions cannot be something eternal. By works or actions here Śaṃkara, of course, means, like Sāṃkhya, the various ritualistic actions as prescribed in the Vedas as well as the *āśrama* duties. He very clearly says in this connection: . . . . "because knowledge subserves the purpose of man, the lighting of the sacrificial fire and similar works which are enjoined on the different *āśramas* are not to be observed, since man's purpose is effected through knowledge."[20] To establish firmly that *Mokṣa* is attainable by knowledge alone, Śaṃkara takes support from the statements of the various Upaniṣads, such as *Chāndogya Up.* III.4.1, VIIII.7.12, *Taittirīya Up.* II.1, *Bṛhadāraṇyaka Up.* IV.5, 6-15 etc.

However, despite the above, Śaṃkara does not consider the ritualistic acts and the *āśrama* duties as absolutely worthless. His point is that they are not indispensable. Still, according to him, if one performs duties prescribed for the *āśramas* as well as the unconditional duties meant for everyone, that would help, rather than hinder, the course towards *Mokṣa*. The performing of such duties will help in effecting *cittaśuddhi* and save the performer from being overpowered by passions.[21] This *cittaśuddhi* and gradual freedom from passions will facilitate the promotion of knowledge.[22] So *dhārmika* duties as auxiliaries may be helpful towards the attainment of *Mokṣa*. They are not to be despised.

In addition to the ritualistic and *āśrama* duties, Śaṃkara also enumerates certain personal virtues such as self-restraint, renunciation, tranquillity, patience and concentration of mind as somewhat more direct means towards knowledge.[23] In support he quotes *Bṛhadāraṇyaka Upaniṣad*: "Therefore he who knows this, having become calm, subdued, satisfied, patient and collected, sees self in self."[24] He further says that calmness of mind is required for the final attainment of knowledge. This shows that Śaṃkara has greater regard for higher virtues of individual morality than for the ritualistic acts and *āśrama* duties, although the latter in his eyes are also of value. Thus although Śaṃkara asserts that *Mokṣa* is attainable through knowledge, he gives due importance and value to both the crude and finer ethical qualities. Evaluating the role of works as means to knowledge Deussen comments, "The works named do not, strictly speaking, produce knoweldge as their fruit, because knowledge is subject to no prescribed rule, and because its fruit (liberation) cannot be brought about by any means. These works are only auxiliaries (*sahkārins*) to the attainment of knowledge in as much as the man who leads a life of holy works is not overpowered by affections (*kleśa*) such as passion etc. According to this their role in the scheme of salvation would not be so much meritorious as ascetic."[25]

(g) *The Rāmānuja Vedānta*

Rāmānuja seems to allow the performance of *dharma* in a wider sense to include all the ritualistic and *āśrama* duties. Duties pertaining to the purer aspects of individual and social morality are also included. In the narrower sense ethical virtues and duties proper as part of *dharma* already play a very vital and substantial role in the path leading to liberation. In fact, he propounds a doctrine of *Mokṣa-sādhana* which very ably includes within it all the three paths of liberation generally recognised in the Indian tradition—the path of *jñāna*, the path of *karma* and the path of *bhakti*. And so his doctrine may very well be called *samuccayavāda*, a doctrine which effectively brings about a *samuccaya* of knowledge, action and devotion to God, all the three. But the details of this *samuccaya* are exposed by Rāmānuja in a manner that gives *dharma* a very prominent role in it.

According to Rāmānuja, knowledge which is finally to give us deliverence is attainable by meditation (*upāsanā*). But this *upāsanā* includes within it steps which are for the most part *dhārmika* or moral in their nature. We have seen all these steps and their elucidation in our Chapter VI. Elements of both individual and social morality have their due places in the moral steps mentioned. Besides the elements of purer morality, Rāmānuja also recommends for inclusion the performance of the *āśrama* and other sacrificial duties. He thinks the process of meditaion that starts from the performance of such duties leads to liberation. We know that action done with attachment are the root cause of bondage. So, first of all such evil actions are to be countered. That can be effected by the performance of prescribed *dhārmika* duties. As Rāmānuja says, "Hence, in order that knowledge may arise, evil works have to be got rid of and this is effected by the performance of acts of religious duty not aiming at some immediate result (such as the heavenly world and the like); according to the text 'by works of religious duty, he discards all evils'. Knowledge which is means of reaching *Brahman* thus requires the work prescribed for the different *āśramas*. . . ."[26] For this Rāmānuja also thinks it necessary to go into the details of Pūrva Mīmāṃsā, which will tell us the kind of works to be done.

It is clear that, according to Rāmānuja, performance of *dharma* is a necessary part of the means to *Mokṣa*. But the devotion to God is most important. Final release is the outcome of the grace of God, and this grace has to be elicited from Him by means of love and devotion to Him with a sense of complete surrender. For establishing the supreme value of *bhakti* for the attainment of liberation, Rāmānuja quotes the *Bhagavadgītā* as saying, "Neither by the Vedas, no by austerities, nor by gifts, nor by sacrifice can I be so seen as thou hast seen me. But by devotion exclusive I may in this form be known and seen in truth, O Arjuna, and also be entered into."[27] Thus performance of duties is necessary, but ultimately it is devotion to God which brings liberation. What Rāmānuja calls *upāsanā* (meditation), he sometimes identifies with *bhakti*, but what he means by *bhakti* is pure love of and complete surrender to God.

(h) ***Buddhism***

In the two heterodox systems of Indian thought—Buddhism and Jainism—*dharma* in the sense of morality proper (individual and social both) has been given a predominant place. The fourth Noble Truth of Buddhism envisages that *Nirvāṇa* is to be attained by following the eightfold discipline. The eightfold discipline is broadly put under three heads—*prajñā*, *śīla* and *samādhi*. It is *śīla* which properly speaking constitutes Buddhist morality. There are three *śīlas*—right speech, right conduct and right livelihood. Right conduct consists of the famous five *śīlas* (*pañcaśīla*) of Buddhism. These five *śīlas* contribute very significantly towards the attainment of *Nirvāṇa*. Buddhism also speaks of eight *śīlas* (*aṭṭha śīla*) and ten *śīlas* (*daśa śīla*) meant for the laiety and the monk respectively for the attainment of *Nirvāṇa*. These *aṭṭha* and *daśa śīlas* include the five *śīlas* mentioned earlier. These *śīlas* include virtues of both individual and social morality, but the former is predominant. To a large extent virtues relating to individual purity have been emphasized. All these things are described in detail in Chapter VI. The only thing to be reasserted here is that morality plays a dominant role in Buddhism in leading us to *Nirvāṇa*. What distinguishes Buddhism from Hindu systems, insofar as the role of *dharma* in *Mokṣa* is concerned, is that the former has absolutely no palce in it for the ceremonial or ritualistic duties. *Dharma* in the sense of morality proper has alone its place in the path leading to *Nirvāṇa*.

(i) ***Jainism***

Jainism has three jewels (*Triratna*) to lead one to liberation. These three jewels are—right faith, right knowledge and right conduct. It is essential to follow all the three for attaining *Mokṣa*, but the last one, i.e., right conduct seems to be the most important. Right conduct is constituted by what is known as *pañcamahāvrata* in Jainism. We have already given a detailed description of it in our Chapter VI and we are not therefore repeating the same. What is to be marked is that morality proper has a very important place in the Jaina theory of liberation. The *Pañcamahāvrata* contains within it elements of both individual and social morality. Besides the five *vratas* coming under *Pañcamahāvrata*, various *anuvratas*, more concerned with individual purity, chastity, renunciation than with elements of social morality, are talked about in Jainism. So like Buddhism, Jainism also lays greater emphasis on virtues of individual purity as a means to attain liberation. Again, like Buddhism, Jainism is also averse to performing ritualistic or ceremonial duties, including sacrifices.

3. General Estimate

A brief survey of the concept of *Mokṣa* and the role of *dharma* (morality) in its attainment in the Indian tradition brings out the role of *dharma* as a pathway to *Mokṣa*. The main emphasis is, however, on *jñāna*. The performance of *dharma* mainly consists, it is said, in the performance of certain actions. Since actions of any kind bind, *dharma* cannot in any way lead to *Mokṣa*. But such narrow interpretation does not convey the true spirit of the Indian tradition. *Karmas* no doubt bind, but only those done with egoistic passions. *Karmas* done with a sense of duty do not bind. So all systems advise doing unconditional *karmas*. Again actions prescribed for one's *āśrama* also cleanse the evil passions to a great extent and make the path to knowledge easier. Perhaps Sāṃkhya is the only system which does not at all recognise the role of these *karmas*. But again Sāṃkhya also recognises the role of purer virtues of individual morality. Mīmāṃsā lays utmost emphasis on the performance of these *dharmas*. No system ignores or minimises the importance of ethical virtues of both individual and social import. Since bondage arises from ignorance, emphasis on *jñāna* is natural in Indian tradition. But the role of morality or *dharma* has not been ignored either. The role of virtues relating to individual morality has naturally received more emphasis. For the attainment of *jñāna*, the virtues of individual purity, self-discipline, renunciation are more relevant and greater emphasis is laid upon their acquisition. Due place has been given to elements of social morality also, specially in the Nyāya-Vaiśeṣika, Rāmānuja Vedānta, Buddhism and Jainism. Also the Vedas, the Upaniṣads and the *Bhagavadgītā* duly recognise the role of social morality in our attainment of the highest goal. It is a different matter that no conceptual or logical relationship exists between Indian cannons of social morality and the highest end *Mokṣa*. But their role is recognised. The contemporary Indian thought rather makes a greater and more logical scope for the elements of social morality to be conducive to *Mokṣa*. This can be seen in our brief consideration of the contemporary Indian ethical thought towards the end of Chapter VI.

REFERENCES

1. *Bṛh. Up.* VI.3.21.
2. *Māṇḍūkya Up.* III.1.40.
3. *Māṇḍūkya Up.* III.1.3.
4. *NS* 1.1.22.
5. *SS* 1.1.
6. *Śāstradīpikā* (Baroda Oriental Institute, 1940), p. 187.
7. *Ibid.*, Introduction.
8. Dr. Ganga Nath Jha, *Pūrva Mīmāṃsā in its Sources* (Banaras Hindu University, 1942), p. 31.
9. *The Dhammapada,* p. 203.
10. S. Radhakrishnan, *Brahma Sūtra,* p. 210.
11. E.W. Hopkins, *Ethics of India,* p. 86.
12. *SS* III.25.
13. *Ibid.*, 1.85.
14. *Ibid.*, III.30.
15. *Ibid.*, III.35.
16. *SV* 110.
17. *Ibid.*, 95.103.
18. *Śāstradīpikā,* Introduction and p. 149.
19. Ganga Nath Jha, *op. cit.*, p. 31.
20. *SB* III.4.25.
21. *Ibid.*, III.4.35.
22. *Ibid.*, III.4.38.
23. *Ibid.*, III.4.27.
24. *Ibid.*, IV.4.23.
25. Deussen, *The System of Vedānta* (Çhicago Open Court, 1912), pp. 411-12.
26. *RB* 1.1.1.
27. *BG* XI.53.54.

CHAPTER X

Ethical and Other Related Concepts

1. *Ṛta*

As we have noted earlier, the concept of *Ṛta* may be regarded as the foundational source of morality in India. In its original form the concept is found to be a repository of cosmic order, specially the order of the heavenly bodies, the day and night and the various seasons. But gradually it puts on a connotation making it a repository of moral order. It is, as a matter of fact, a three-pronged order—a cosmic order, a ritualistic order and a moral order—all at the same time. But still it is a unitary principle. Not only it is a unity in each of the three spheres, rather it is a unity throughout them all. Each of the three orders—natural, sacrificial and moral—is a manifestation of the same universal *Ṛta*.

'*Ṛta*' is taken to have come out of the root 'R' which is supposed to have two primary groups of meanings. It signifies 'to move' and (through movement) 'to fit or to arrange'. Thus movement or activity and order or organisation (including law) seem to be the two basic elements constituting the Vedic concept of *Ṛta*. Everything in the universe which shows activity and law and order through activity may be said to have *Ṛta* for its underlying principle.

Ṛta is not merely a statutory or regulative principle, it is objective. It is imbibed or incorporated in the very constitution of the universe. The law and order in every sphere is a manifestation of this *Ṛta*. Along with *satya* and *tapas*, it is regarded as one of the primal constituents of the universe.[1] It is regarded as a world-embracing power.[2] Thus *Ṛta* is objective and real. In a sense it is ideal too. It is ideal in the sense that, as far as the world of space and time is concerned, it is not actually given there. It works in a subtle and intangible manner. However, it is in the sphere of human conduct that its ideal nature can be most clearly marked. *Ṛta* sets an ideal here with reference to which the distinction between 'is' and 'ought' or 'right' and 'wrong' assumes some meaning. As we have seen earlier also, it sets the moral point of view in motion. It is said that *Ṛta* is merely a principle of (moral) order which simply implies that there is no caprice or disorder in the realm of morality: good acts yield good results and the bad acts the bad ones.

It is on this basic comprehensive principle implied by *Ṛta* that the famous law of *karma,* regarded as a fundamental presupposition of Indian ethics, is based. All this is correct, but to take *Ṛta* as merely a principle of order having no content of right or wrong within itself is wrong. It is taken in the Vedas as a principle of righteousness or goodness as is clear from what is expressly stated in the *Ṛg Veda*: "The wicked travel not the path way of *Ṛta*."[3] This is also clear from the fact that the opposite of *Ṛta* has been taken in the Vedas as *Anṛta*, which means *pāpa* or evil. *Ṛta* thus stands for the principle of good.

But what, after all, this good or righteousness of *Ṛta* consist in? What exactly is its moral content which makes it a principle of goodness or righteousness? What are the moral qualities included within it? Perhaps there is no clear answer to such questions in the Veda. Although *Ṛta* stands for moral order as well as for virtue and righteousnes, one hardly gathers any clear hint from the Vedas as to what moral qualities constitute the contents of the *Ṛta* so that a life led in the light of them will be called a life led according to *Ṛta*. The only such indication that we find is that *Ṛta* is so often identified with truth. *Ṛta* is sometimes spoken of as an independent principle, independent of any god or goddess, but sometimes gods are regarded as its guardian. Of all gods, however, Varuṇa is pre-eminently regarded as the guardian of *Ṛta* and as the god of truth. Indra is presented as addressing Varuṇa in the following manner:

> But thou, O Varuṇa, if thou dost love me,
> O king, discerning truth and right from falsehood,
> Come and be Lord and Ruler of my kingdom.[4]

Varuṇa being the custodian of *Ṛta* as well as a god of truth, it seems very likely that *Ṛta* has a nearness to truth. Not only that, sometimes *Ṛta* or the eternal moral law seems to be identified with truth. For instance, in the *Ṛg Veda* it is said "All falsehood, Mitrā-Varuṇa, ye conquer, and closely cleave unto the Law Eternal."[5] Truth, as a matter of fact, is regarded as the very foundation of the universe, and so also the Eternal Law, the *Ṛta*.

Truth is therefore the only moral quality to constitute the content of *Ṛta*. A life according ro *Ṛta* may therefore be called veracious or truthful.

Nothing more is indicated by way of the righteous nature of *Ṛta*. By and large, it stands out as a principle of order, specially of moral order.

Perhaps the above account of *Ṛta* makes it clear that although it is the foundational source of morality in India, it by itself can hardly be regarded as a moral principle. It is a principle of order which guarantees that there is no caprice or arbitrariness in the moral world. But it hardly gives us any criterion to distinguish between right and wrong, moral and immoral. It is said that a life of righteousness is a life according to the *Ṛta*, but where does one find the criterion from to distinguish between a righteous and unrighteous? It will perhaps be found in a criterion ulterior to that of *Ṛta*. *Ṛta* by itself can hardly give us any such criterion. If at all it can give us anything by way of providing a criterion, it is in the form of truth as a virtue. So whatever is truthful is in accordance with the *Ṛta* and hence righteous. Nothing more can be said about a life of righteousness on the basis of *Ṛta*. In this way, if it is to be regarded as a moral principle, at most it can provide us with only one criterion of righteousness and that is in the form of truth. Thus although *Ṛta* gives us an idea about the possible moral way of life, it hardly gives any idea about the actual nature of moral life.

2. *Dharma*

The word '*dharma*' comes from the verbal root '*dhṛ*' which means 'to hold', 'to sustain', or 'to support'. Thus *dharma* stands for the individual essence of objects or for the inner law by which they are sustained or supported. So often its connotation extends from individual objects to the entire universe. Thus *dharma* becomes the inner principle which sustains or holds together the entire universe. In this sense it comes very near to *Ṛta*, at least insofar as the latter is a principle of cosmic order.

But again like *Ṛta*, *dharma* also has not only a cosmic dimension, but a moral dimension too. In that aspect *dharma* denotes a moral base of the universe without which it (the universe) will distintegrate or fall apart. But again in this sense '*dharma*' implies not only moral virtues or duties, but the whole set of customs, laws, rules, rituals, religious beliefs and practices recognised as approved or settled in the society for people to follow. It is by the observance of all these that the social fabric or the entire universe is supposed to be sustained or held together. '*Dharma*' is thus a term of very wide import in the Indian setting. No English word can be exactly equivalent to it. What John Mckenzie writes in special reference to the use of the term '*dharma*' in the Dharma sūtras, seems to me to characterise aptly the difficulty in translating it in any one way, such as, religion or law or morality or the like. The term *'dharma'* says Mckenzie, "is variously translated as Religion, Virtue, Law, Duty. All these words convey something of the meaning, but to use any one of them as an equivalent is highly misleading. Much confusion might be avoided if it were recognised once for all that the term *'dhama'*, as used at any rate in the Dharma sūtras, was applied to a condition of things to which modern terms like religion, virtue and law are strictly speaking inapplicable. In India in those days no clear distinction was drawn between moral and religious duties, usages, customary observance and law, and *dharma* was the term which was applied to the whole complex of forms of conduct that were settled or established."[6]

Similarly K.V. Rangaswami Aiyangar writes regarding the various senses in which the term *'dharma'* has been used in the ancient Indian tradition, "*'Dharma'* is used in so many senses that it eludes definition. It stands for nature, intrinsic quality, civil and moral law, justice, virtue, merit, duty and morality."[7] In a similar vein, P.S. Sivaswamy Aiyer remarks: "the contents of *dhama*, as evidenced by its use in the various treatises on *dharma*, are virtually coextensive with the entire sphere of human behaviour and whose numerous and vital prescripts descend to the minutest details of life and conduct."[8]

The above references and many more that can be brought about amply show that the term *'dharma'* as used in the Indian philosophical, religious or ethical tradition is very broad and comprehensive. However, it has been prominently taken in the sense of moral law which sustains and maintains the entire universe. As manifested in the human realm, it is a set of virtues and duties that man must follow. By the *dharma* of a man is generally meant his duties or obligations towards others, towards himself and also towards the deities. Thus the duties or virtues enumerated under *dharma* are not always, strictly speaking, moral duties or virtues; they also include, for example, duties in respect of health, knowledge etc. as well as the various ritualistic duties. But under Indian concept of morality, which includes both personal and social morality, they may all in a broad sense be called moral duties or virtues.

Dharma, as understood in the above sense, (i.e. in the sense of duties, obligations and virtues to be inculcated or carried out by human beings) has generally been recognised to be of two kinds: (1) those which are to be carried out by each and every man irrespective of his station in life, and (2) those which are to be observed by a man by virtue of his having a particular station in life—both in respect of social and individual life. The first is known as *sādhāraṇa dharma* and the second as *varṇāśrama dharma. Sādhāraṇa dharmas* are general duties to be performed by each and evey human being by virtue of his being a human. Such duties may also be called common or universal duties because they are to be performed by each and evey human being, irrespective of his age, caste or creed. They are obligatory on man as man and not because of his being at any particular stage of life. Various ancient Indian thinkers differ among themselves in presenting the list of the *sādhāraṇa dharmas,* but by and large *dharmas* such as *satya, asteya, ahiṃsā,* hospitality, compassion, *indriya-nigraha, akrodha* (absence of anger) etc. have been recognised as *sādhāraṇa dharmas* in the Indian tradition. The *varṇāśrama dharmas* are duties relative to the *varṇa* or class to which one belongs in the society and to the *āśrama* or stage of life through which one is passing at a particular time. There are four *varṇas—Brāhmaṇa, kṣatriya, Vaiśya* and *Śūdra*—and four *āśramas—Brahmacarya, Gārhasthya, Vanaprastha* and *Sannyāsa*—recognised by the Indian tradition, and there are *dharmas* or duties prescribed relative to each and every *varṇa* or *āśrama.*

Every individual has to observe the *dharma* or *dharmas* relative to the *varṇa* or *āśrama* to which he belongs. The observance of the *varṇāśrama dharma* by any one has been taken as the observance of one's *svadharma.* The observance of this *svadharma* has been accorded great importance in the Indian tradition, especially in the *Bhagavadgītā.* According to the *Bhagavadgītā,* it seems that the observance of *svadharma* has been emphasized to such an extent that at the time of a possible conflict between *varṇāśrama dharma* and *sādhāraṇa dharma,* it is the former which is to prevail over the latter. This can very well be seen in Lord Kṛṣṇa's unequivocal advice to Arjuna to resort to *hiṃsā* without any hesitation for the observance of *svadharma,* i.e., the *dharma* appropriate for a *kṣatriya.* It is clearly said in the *Gītā* that it is always better to observe one's own *dharma* (*svadharma*) than following the *dharma* of others.[9]

In the Indian scheme of *puruṣārthas, dharma* is given a very prominent place. In the theory of *trivarga,* it is given the highest place, but in that of *caturvarga* it is *Mokṣa* which is given the highest place, and *dharma* is generally regarded merely as a means to *Mokṣa.* In any case, however, its role is very important insofar as the observance of *dharma* is necessary for any and every human being even while pursuing the goals of *kāma* and *artha,* the two lower *puruṣārthas.* The underlying idea is that *dharma* is the foundation of human society, nay, of the universe itself. It is strengthened by every man's observance of his own *dharma* sincerely and honestly. If *dharma* suffers, everything is destroyed. As Manu says, "*Dharma* being violated, destroyes, *dharma* being preserved, preserves. Therefore, *dharma* must not be violated, lest violated *dharma* may destroy us."[10] More about the status of *dharma* in the scheme of *puruṣārthas,* we shall bring forth while dealing with the concept of *puruṣārtha* a few pages ahead.

That '*dharma*' is a very comprehensive term and cannot be attributed only with some moral connotation in all its usages is clear. At least in the sense of the property of the objects or even in the sense of their inner essential principle which make them stand as they are, '*dharma*' has nothing to do with morality. But we have seen moral law is manifested in human realm in terms of the various prescribed duties and virtues for man. Even in this sense we find that '*dharma*' has got a much wider connotation to encompass within itself even duties not ordinarily regarded moral by man. For instance, in Manu's list of *dharmas*, knowledge and learning (*dhi* and *vidyā*) as well as cleanliness (*śauca*) are also included. These may be regarded as duties concerning mental development and health, but they seem to do nothing with what we ordinarily regard as moral duties.

Similarly, rituals and other duties directed towards gods and goddesses also are included under *dharma.* These may be called religious duties, but not the moral ones. As a matter of fact, under *dharma* are prescribed all sorts of duties which relate to almost all aspects of man's life, such as, duties of a husband towards his wife and *vice versa,* duties of a king to his subjects and *vice versa* etc. Ordinarily speaking, all these cannot be regarded as moral duties. In the Indian concept of morality are included not only virtues and duties of social obligation, but also individual virtues and duties leading to the control of senses, *cittaśuddhi.* All duties relating to bodily purity (*śauca*), knowledge etc. as well as ritualistic duties relating to gods and goddesses contribute towards personal upliftment and purity of mind and heart (*cittaśuddhi*). In that broad sense all are treated as moral duties. It is in that broad sense only that *āśrama dharmas* can be regarded as moral duties. So, in a sense, whatever individual and social duties men are supposed to perform have been regarded as man's *dharmas* by the Indian tradition. They are all regarded as men's moral duties. In this way, whatever contributes in any way towards man's development of a balanced life on the path of spirituality is regarded as *dhārmika* or moral in the Indian context. In that sense, all laws of individual and social living are regarded as prescriptions of moral duties.

'*Dharma*' has been taken in the Indian tradition also in the sense of merit (or demerit) that one earns due to his good (or bad) duties. In this sense *dharma* refers to the *saṃkāras* that one accumulates due to his own *karmas* and which are utimately responsible for his rebirth. In this sense '*dharma*' does not refer to moral virtues or duties, but it is certainly related to them. Merit is the result of virtuous *karmas* while demerit (*adharma* or bad *saṃskāras*) is the result of the acts of vice. So, in that sense also *dharma* has got a moral implication. Notwithstanding its by and large wide connotation, *dharma* is equated with morality in the Indian context. What should be remembered is that the term 'morality' itself is being understood here in a very wide context, and is not to be equated with its narrow use in the Western context.

3. *Karma*

'*Karma*' literally means action of any kind done by human beings. But actions which are morally significant are known as voluntary actions or *aicchika karmas*. Here by '*karma*' we will mean only such actions and will try to make an analysis of them in Indian setting with special reference to what is known as the law of *karma*.

Karmas, according to Indian thinkers, owe their origin either to *rāga* or to *dveṣa*. *Rāga* is, generally speaking, desire to own or possess pleasure-giving objects and *dveṣa* is the desire to avoid objects which are deemed to cause pain and suffering. In other words, *rāga* is the sense of attachment with the pleasurable objects, while *dveṣa* consists in the sense of detachment or repulsion from the painful objects. Both kinds of actions are to be known as desireful actions or *aicchika karmas*. Such *karmas*, according to Indian thinkers, unfailingly generate effects or consequences which have their bearings on the life of the doer. This belief is deeply engrained in the Hindu, the Bauddha and Jaina traditions. The famous law of *karma*, one of the fundamental postulates of Indian theory of morals, owes its origin to this belief. Let us see the meaning and implications of this law of *karma*.

The law of *karma*, in the first instance, may be taken as an extension of the law of causation to the sphere of human conduct. It is an extension of the law of causation in the sense that every action that a man does has its necessary consequences or, in the other words, every action serves as a cause for some effects. These effects do not expand or vanish in the world at large; they have their necessary and unfailing bearing on the future state of things to come in the life of the doer. Whatever happiness or sorrow one undergoes in this life are the necessary results of actions in his past life. So, he is undergoing only such happiness or sorrow to which he is entitled by virtue of his past deeds. The 'past' refers as much to the 'past' of the present life as to the 'past' of a supposedly earlier birth. In other words, whatever consequences in terms of happiness or sorrow one is undergoing at present are not necessarily the results of his deeds in the recent past, rather they might be the consequences of a remote past life.

With the doctrine of *karma* is associated a belief in the past and future lives expressed in the doctrine of rebirth. A chain of causation, which links our actions and our status in any particular life, is formed. The state-of-affairs that one is facing in one's present life including, of course, the present life itself, is determined by one's actions in the past life or lives and the state-of-affairs that are awaiting him in his future life including the future life itself will be the consequences of his deeds in the present life. Thus actions done by a person produce for him good or bad results in accordance with his good or bad actions. Such results are not necessarily produced in the immediate future. They may be produced after a long time, even after the end of the present life. Explaining how an action produces its effect after such a long time, Indian thinkers maintain that every action done produces a *saṃskāra* or a potency. This potency is never lost or destroyed (*kṛtapraṇāśa*) and when ripened or matured it produces appropriate consequences for the doer of the action to experience.

This leads us to the second important feature of the law of *karma* and that is its comparison with the physical law of the conservation of energy. On the parity of the above physical law, the law of *karma* may be taken as the law of the conservation of moral values. The law of the conservation of energy is the law to the effect that no energy in the world is ever lost, it is simply transformed in some other form. In a similar vein, the law of *karma* says that no action ever passes for nothing, no action is ever lost in vain. Every action is bound to produce its natural result and the doer of the action is bound to bear its burden. What is done is never lost in vain (*kṛtapraṇāśa*). This is the law of the conservation of moral values. Another aspect of the law is that one never comes across any result which is not of his own action (*akṛtābhyupagama*). One undergoes consequences only because he deserves them by virtue of his own actions. The world, governed by the law of *karma*, is a moral world with complete justice in the award of reward and punishment, happiness and suffering. The law of *karma* in this sense is the law of retribution. One gets only what he deserves in return of his own actions. He is neither held responsible for the actions done by others nor he has to undergo the consequence of such actions. There is complete justice, and no anarchy, in the moral world. The doer of good actions experiences happiness and the doer of bad actions pain and suffering. There is no deviation from this law under any condition. As Radhakrishnan says. "According to the principle of *karma* there is nothing uncertain or capricious in the moral world. We reap what we sow."[11] In an identical spirit Prof. Hiriyanna remarks, "Whatever we knowingly do, will sooner or later, bring us the result we merit; and there is no way of escape from it. What we sow, we must reap."[12]

The law of *karma* envisages that no action done ever goes unrewarded or unpunished. Three kinds of *karmas—prārabdha, sañcita* and *sañcīyamāna*—to which the law applies are recognised in Indian thought. The effect of the first one can in no way be evaded or got rid of. The effects of the two latter *karmas* can be avoided by the attainment of true knowledge (or in the case of the Mīmāṃsakas, by the sincere performance of *nityanaimittika karmas*). Actions which were done in the past life and whose *saṃskāras* have matured to produce effects are known as *prārabdha karmas*. Actions which were done previously but whose *saṃskāras* have not yet matured for producing effects are known as *sañcita karamas* and those actions which are being done presently or currently and whose *saṃskāras* are still further from attaining maturity for producing effects are known as *sañcīyamāna karmas. Prārabdha karmas* are ripe *karmas* which are bound to produce effects, but if one makes sincere efforts by way of doing the *nityanaimittika karmas* or by attaining true knowledge, he can check *sañcita* and *sañcīyamāna karmas* from producing effects.

As we have indicated above, the concept of *karma* is essentially bound up with the concept of rebirth in Indian philosophy. The law of *karma*, we have seen, says that one is bound to undergo the consequences of one's action. Now, if one does not exhaust the consequences of his action in this life, he has to be reborn for undergoing them. But rebirth is bondage. Thus actions of all kinds, whether good or bad, bind. Good actions, no doubt, yield good results and consequently elevated rebirth, but rebirth nevertheless. Hence good and bad actions bind and cause rebirth. Both generate potencies which in due course yield results for the doer to undergo either in this life or in the life beyond. For going beyond the shackles of the law of *karma* and of rebirth, therefore, it is necessary to do *niṣkāma karmas*, which do not generate any *saṃskāras* for future rebirth and bondage. We shall deal with the concept of *niṣkāma karma* separately in the following pages.

It is to be seen from the above that the principle of *karma* as it has been understood in the Indian tradition cannot be a moral principle. It does not tell us anything about what is right and what is wrong. It simply tells us that right actions are rewarded by good results and wrong actions by bad results. That is the principle of retribution, not of morality. The law of *karma,* therefore, may be a presupposition or postulate of morality, but it is not by itself a principle of morality.

The law of *karma* is regarded as the law of causation extended in the moral world. But by that it does not become a moral law. It remains a law of causation all the same, related to moral matters. It is interpreted as working mechanically as a principle of order in the moral world and nothing else. With the guarantee that moral acts will be rewarded by good results and immoral acts by bad ones, it upholds morality and so serves as the basis of it, but does not provide by itself any criterion for distinguishing between what is moral and what is immoral. If it is said that by uniting moral acts with good results and immoral acts with bad ones, it provides us with a criterion in a retrospective manner, it may be pointed out that no such criterion is provided to a non-consequentialist for whom something is moral simply because it is so, and not because of its consequence.

4. *Niṣkāma Karma*

Actions which bind us and cause rebirth are those done with some desire. So actions which come under the sway of the law of *karma* are those which are done with the conscious desire of achieving something. Such actions are also known as attached actions, or actions done with some attachment. *Niṣkāma karmas,* on the contrary, are actions done without any attachment, i.e., without any conscious intention of achieving something. In other words, actions done without any *rāga* or *dveṣa* are non-attached actions. Conceptually, non-attached actions are actions completely devoid of any desire, whether the desire be egoistic or altruistic, secular or religious, material or spiritual. But in Indian thought it seems that non-attachment or 'desirelessness' means the absence of only the narrow egoistic desires. An action may be non-attached even when the doer does it with the aim of promoting public welfare or of attaining the spiritual goal of *Mokṣa* or freedom. What is prohibited or enjoined to be given up is the inculcation of worldly aspirations, the mundane egoistic interests, and not the higher ends like social preservation or self-purification and self-realisation. This is clear from the following ideas of the *Gītā* on *karma-yoga:* "As the unlearned act from attachment to their work, so should the learned also act, O Bhārata, but without any attachment, with the desire to maintain the world-order."[13] And again, "The yogins perform works merely with the body, mind, understanding or merely with the senses, abandoning attachment, for the purification of their souls."[14] So, if the goal is a higher one like the maintenance of the world-order, or the purification of the soul, the action remains a non-attached one. As a matter of fact, in the Indian thinking only such actions are attached actions and cause bondage which are done under the influence of *avidyā* (ignorance), and such actions are only those actions which are prompted by *rāga* and *dveṣa*. Again actions prompted by *rāga* and *dveṣa* are all meant for attaining worldly pleasure and avoiding worldly pain. So, only such desires which are meant for worldly pleasure and avoidance of worldly pain are to be abandoned. In other words, acts done with egoistic passions are attached actions. Those which do not concern narrow egoistic ends, but refer to altruistic or higher spiritual ends, are not to be construed as attached actions even if there is some desire behind them.

The ideal of *niṣkāma karma* may be taken as a synthesis between what has been called *pravṛtti* and *nivṛtti* in the Indian ethical system. *Pravṛtti* is the path of active life with the object of attaining heaven or some such state of happiness. Thus *pravṛtti* refers to desireful actions, the desire being happiness in the present life or happiness in heaven. Such acts include all the rituals and ceremonies prescribed in the Vedas or other Śāstras. Such acts are definitely therefore attached actions. As opposed to *pravṛtti, nivṛtti* is the path of total renunciation of works. It is a quietistic path, taking *sādhanā, samādhi* etc. as the sole pathway to salvation. The essential thing involved herein is that for salvation one has to renounce the world and worldly activities completely and has to take recourse to what is known as *jñāna-mārga* or the path of knowledge. The doctrine of *niṣkāma karma* cuts a middle course between the above two extreme pathways. It holds that what is required for liberation is not the renunciation of world or worldly actions, but the renunciation only of *kāma* (passion or egoistic desire). The *Gītā* clearly says that actions are to be done; nobody can remain without performing actions. So renunciation of works is not required. What is required is renunciation in action. That is, even in spite of doing action, one is not to be involved in the fruit of the action. His concern is work and work alone, and never the fruit thereof. The famous *Gītā* saying in this regard is as follows: "To action alone hast thou a right and never at all to its fruits; let not the fruits of action be they motive; neither let there be in thee any attachment to inaction."[15] Thus *niṣkāma karma* is neither *naiskarmya* (inaction) nor *karma* (action) with an eye upon the fruit thereof. In other words, it is neither *nivṛtti* nor *pravṛtti.* It is action without attachment to the fruits thereof.

The above noted reference from the *Gītā* puts forth one more important aspect of the doctrine of *niṣkāma karma*. One should renounce the fruit of his action not because desire for the fruits bind but, rather more importantly, because fruits of actions are not within the power of the doer, they are not his right at all. Fruits are within the power or control of God. So, why keep an eye on that which is not within your power? The *Gītā*, therefore, advises us the ideal of *niṣkāma karma* that one should act with a sense of complete surrender to God, with an utter sense of resigning or offering all works to God. "He who works, having given up attachment, resigning his actions to God, is not touched by sin, even as a lotus leaf (is untouched) by water."[16] Kṛṣṇa, the Lord, exhorts Arjuna to give up his *moha*, in the following words: "Resigning all thy works to Me, with thy consciousness fixed in the self, being free from desire and egoism, fight, delivered from thy fever."[17] Thus, according to the *Bhagavadgītā*, the ideal of *niṣkāma karma* is realised by performing selfless actions, surrendering fruits of actions to God.

This doesn't, however, mean that in the atheistic systems of India there is no place for *niṣkāma karma*. As a matter of fact, systems like Buddhism, Mīmāṃsā etc., which are atheistic systems, have also ample place and importance for *niṣkāma karma*. Buddha compares *niṣkāma karmas* to fried seeds which do not germinate. Like fried seed, actions done without attachment do not generate any *saṃskāra* and consequently do not bind. Similarly, the *nitya-naimittika karmas* of the Mīmāṃsakas are to be taken as *niṣkāma karmas*, because these *karmas* are to be performed according to them by everyone without any consideration for anything other than one's *dharma* or duty. As a matter of fact, one very important dimension of *niṣkāma karma* is its giving vent to the ideal of duty for duty's sake. If one's right or power is limited to action alone, and not to the result, then he has to do his assigned action only with the sense of duty and with no other consideration. Placed in the world as we are, we have certain duties to perform. And we are to perform these duties simply for the sake of duties. We have to do them, because we are obliged to do them as our assigned *dharmas*. *Niṣkāma karma* is not inaction, it is action *par excellence*. But again it is action for no selfish gain, for no desired end. Then action what for? For action sake alone. We have to act, because we are to act. We have been assigned certain duties by virtue of being men and also by virtue of being placed in the world with a certain status in life. We have to perform these assigned duties with the full sense of duty and for nothing else. This is nothing but duty for duty's sake. So *niṣkāma karma* implies within it duty for duty sake. It is a fact that all actions, whether desireful or desireless, bear their natural fruits but the fruits of the latter have no binding effect upon the doer; they have a liberating effect rather.

It is clear from the above that what binds, and consequently what is the real cause of rebirth and suffering, is *kāma* (attachment) and not *karma* (action). But the question is: Is non-attached action necessarily moral and the attached action necessarily immoral? The answer will be evidently negative, because the question of morality is associated with actions which are done by *rāga* and *dveṣa*. It is these which are the natural springs of action whether moral or immoral, right or wrong. So the concept of *niṣkāma karma* seems to be a morally neutral concept. An action like killing will be regarded as wrong, whether it be done with attachment or with complete sense of non-attachment. Similarly, if one acts for the good of others even with a sense of attachment it will be appreciated as a right or moral action. It may be pointed out here that purely altruistic actions done even with a sense of attachment for achieving the altruistic goal is treated as non-attached action for all practical purposes in the Indian tradition. So, action done for the good of others cannot be cited as an example of attached action. But here it is to be seen that actions sometimes done even with a sense of personal or egoistic interest may not necessarily be regarded as wrong or immoral. For example, nobody would regard the action of wife for the good health of her husband an immoral act, even if it is done with an egoistic end in view. So, the concept of *niṣkāma karma*, regarded as the backbone of Indian ethical thought, is not a moral concept at all, it is rather a morally neutral concept.

But let us turn to the Indian context in which the concept of *niṣkāma karma* is used and understood. Ordinarily, in the light of true *niṣkāmatā* (state of non-attachment), even an act of *hiṃsā* done with a complete sense of detachment will be deemed superior to the act of a wife for her husband with a sense of attachment. But the spirit in which *niṣkāma karma* has been understood in the Indian tradition will perhaps not allow situations like the above. A person who has become really passionless, a *sannyāsī* for example, can never be expected to perform an act of *hiṃsā* or such other ordinarily regarded immoral act. He himself, is, of course above any kind of moral evaluation or distinction. This does not mean he has got a license for doing immoral acts. The nature and character of true *niṣkāma karmī* is such that only good acts follow out of his nature quite automatically. The concept of *niṣkāma karma* is not based on such adhocism that a man can perform at one time with a sense of detachment and at another time with a sense of attachment. Non-attached actions in the true sense of the term are possible only when passionlessness becomes the inherent trait of one's character. In that sense the truly passionless fellow will hardly ever do any morally wrong work. Again, as we have seen, *niṣkāma karma,* as understood in the Indian tradition, does not prohibit actions done with altruistic desires or with higher spiritual aims. It simply prohibits actions which are done with narrow egoistic passions. Mostly such actions will come under the morally wrong category. There may yet be certain actions, for example, the action of a wife for the good health of her husband, which even in spite of being surcharged with egoistic passions cannot be regarded as morally wrong. But here one must remember the total context in which the idea of *niṣkāma karma* is brought in on the Indian scene.

It is not a matter of judging this or that action done with passion as moral or immoral. It is a matter of assuming total outlook for the things and attractions of the world. So far as one works on the practical level, act of a wife for her husband or of a lover for her beloved, or of a son for his father done with attachment may not be considered bad, but the point is that these acts preserve symptoms which are not appreciable from a broader point of view. The ideal of *niṣkāma karma* is a counsel for enlarging one's outlook in which one does not feel his responsibilities only limited to father, son, wife, husband etc., but to all, to the entire society, to the whole cosmos of innumerable creatures. For attaining higher spiritual goal, one has to rise beyond the circle of 'mine' and 'thine' and has to work for the welfare of all. That will be really working in the spirit of *niṣkāma karma.* It is true that a *niṣkāma karmī* is a supermoral being, but he is not amoral; only the sphere of his actions is broadened. Conceptually speaking, *niṣkāmatā* transcends the stage of morality, but then it cannot be regarded as a license for immoral actions. There is rather involved in its spirit a natural inclination for such acts which are morally excellent. Instead of egoistic passions, it gives credence to altruistic and spiritualistic aims.

It may be pointed out here that Kṛṣṇa, the Lord, himself was conselling Arjuna to fight war against his kins on the plea that killing the enemy in war with a sense of detachment was no sin. But killing one's kin is on the face of it a sinful action. Kṛṣṇa was counselling Arjuna that no sin would be committed by him if he killed all his cousins in the war. So non-attachment implies actions which may be ordinarily taken as morally wrong. But here one forgets that non-attachment was not the only plea that Kṛṣṇa was invoking for instigating Arjuna to do the act of killing, it was mixed with the plea of *svadharma*. Arjuna as a *kṣatriya* had to follow his *svadharma* of fighting and killing those who stood in the battlefield as his enemies, and this *svadharma* he was being advised to follow with non-attachment. So his act here could not be regarded as wrong or immoral at all. In the Indian context, the question of moral or immoral acts is to be judged or ascertained in the light of the *svadharma* that one is obliged to follow. The same act may be morally right with respect to one *varṇa* or *āśrama* while completely otherwise for another *varṇa* or *āśrama*. So, it cannot be said that Kṛṣṇa was advising Arjuna to perform a morally wrong act on the plea of *niṣkāmatā*.

The overall spirit of *niṣkāma karma*, as understood in the Indian tradition, therefore, is neither amoral nor morally neutral, although purely conceptually it may be taken to be so.

5. *Puruṣārtha*

'*Puruṣārtha*' literally means the end or goal to be aimed at by people. It may also be taken to mean the end or goal that is actually aimed at or desired by men. In fact, the fourfold classification of *puruṣārtha* lends support to both the meanings. After elaboration of the meanings of these *puruṣārthas*, we shall see that while the first two are such ends which can be taken as actually aimed at by people, the latter two are such which ought to be aimed at by every human being. Let us first, therefore, see the individual meanings of the four *puruṣārthas:*

Kāma: The term actually means desire, but in the scheme of *puruṣārthas*, it means sensuous enjoyment or satisfaction of desires. This satisfaction of sensuous desires includes sexual desire also, besides all other kinds of sensuous desires. The inclusion of *kāma* within *puruṣārthas* actually shows the sensitiveness of the Indian thinkers towards one of the very basic needs of human life. After all, human beings are also in one sense animals—of course, very elevated sort of animals. So, for a balanced development of human life, it is necessary that animal appetites of man are also satisfied. If such desires and appetites are suppressed, there is possibility of abnormality to develop and man will not be fit for higher pursuits. So, by including *kāma* under *puruṣārtha*, the Indian thinkers have recognised the need for human beings to aim at the satisfaction of animal appetites. For proper and well-rounded development of man satisfaction of such appetites may be legitimate.

Artha: This refers to riches, property or material well-being. This is a goal which every normal human being aims at. But, according to the

Indian thinkers, it is not that *artha* is simply aimed at by people, under certain limits it ought to be looked for by them also. For, people in penury can hardly act for higher ends. We saw above that the satisfaction of sensuous desires is a necessary part of normal human life, but for that also *artha* is necessary. So *artha* is a *puruṣārtha* both in the sense that people actually aim at it, and also in the sense that under certain legitimate bounds they ought to aim at it. What is prohibited in the Indian tradition is the unlimited hankering after the accumulation of material wealth. That can certainly not be taken as a *puruṣārtha*. But, under legitimate limits, pursuit after wealth has never been decried in India. As Radhakrishnan says, "There was never in India a national ideal of poverty or squalor. Spiritual life finds full scope only in communities of a certain degree of freedom from sordidness. Lives that are strained and starved cannot be religious except in a rudimentary way. Economic insecurity and individual freedom do not go together."[18]

Dharma: We have seen that *dharma* in its connotation is very broad and indeterminate and may be taken as the very foundation of everything. But in the context of *puruṣārthas*, it generally means the *sāmānya* and *viśeṣa dharmas* which every individual has to follow in virtue of his being a man as well as his having a specific status in life. The life of *dharma* has been consistently given a very high place in Indian tradition. But generally speaking *dharma* is not an end in itself but a means to an end. It brings about a disciplined control over the unlimited and unfettered gratification of the senses. As common man is generally disposed to attain wealth and sensuous pleasure on which *dharma* imposes a briddle, *dharma* is not as a matter of fact generally aimed at. But then it ought to be resorted to by every man in virtue of his being a man. There are certain virtues and duties in accordance with *dharma* which every individual has to inculcate and observe as a matter of bounden duty. So *dharma* is a *puruṣārtha* to be aimed at.

But there is a speciality in *dharma* as *puruṣārtha*. It is not simply that as an independent *puruṣārtha* it is to be aimed at and followed. It is a *puruṣārtha* which permeates and pervades both *kāma* and *artha* in the sense that one is to follow and aim at *kāma* and *artha* only under the regulation and guidance of *dharma*. Only such *kāma* and *artha* are to be pursued which are permitted by *dharma*, i.e., which are in conformity with the *dhārmika* prescriptions. *Dharma* maintains the social fabric, its stability and harmony. By providing a set of norms it helps society move in a disciplined and harmonious manner. So, for the smooth working of the social fabric as well as for preparing oneself for higher pursuits, the observance of the norms set by *dharma* is necessary. Naturally, *artha* and *kāma* are also to be pursued under the overall supervision and guidance of *dharma*.

Mokṣa: This is regarded as the highest *puruṣārtha*, i.e., the highest goal or value of life. This is the value which ought to be aimed at by everybody, although in normal living hardly anybody ever thinks about it or aims at it. *Kāma* and *artha* have been allowed as pursuable goals, but they are not the final goals. They have been allowed in the Indian tradition only insofar as their attainment helps man to develop a normal and balanced life so that he may prepare himself with a sound body and mind for higher spiritual end like *Mokṣa*. This is why *kāma* and *artha* have been advised to be pursued always under the yoke of *dharma*. The observance of *dharma* and the pursuance of *kāma* and *artha* under the yoke of *dharma* prepares man for the pursuance of the highest goal, which is known by the various names of *Mokṣa, Kaivalya, Nirvāṇa*, spiritual freedom, self-realisation etc. *Dharma* is thus regarded by most of the Indian thinkers as a means to *Mokṣa*, and not an end in and by itself.

Mokṣa has been conceived variously under various systems of Indian thought, but certain ideas about it are common. It is a spiritual goal after the attainment of which one gets rid of all kinds of suffering as well as from the cycle of birth and rebirth, which is at the root of all sufferings. Naturally, by the attainment of *Mokṣa*, one becomes free from all sorts of passions and desires which bind. But for most of the systems of Indian philosophy, *Mokṣa* is not only a negative status in which certain things are removed or got rid of. It is a positive state also. It is a state of eternal peace, equanimity and bliss. There are, of course, differences on this score, but this may be taken, by and large, as the general position.

The whole idea of *Mokṣa* is based on the Indian conception of man. Barring Cārvāka, every Indian system believes that man is not essentially as he outwardly looks to be,-i.e., a mere psychophysical being. Within his inner being, there is a spiritual entity, called soul, which is the essential and real being of man. This soul is eternal and does not end with the death of the body. Being a victim of ignorance, it suffers and transmigrates. But by the attainment of true knowledge, it attains liberation or *Mokṣa*. *Mokṣa* is man's highest goal, because after this he gets rid of continuous transmigration. He becomes then established as an eternal spiritual reality in perfect peace and equanimity.

The above are the four *puruṣārthas* recognised by Indian tradition. Of these, the last and the highest one is spiritual but purely personal goal. It is for personal redemption from all kinds of worldly sufferings so that one may rest in permanent peace, that one aims or ought to aim at such a goal. The other three, however, are in an important sense social goals. *Kāma* on the face seems to be a personal goal, becuase what one actually pursues here is the satisfaction of his personal desires. But because *kāma* has to work under the yoke of *dharma*, it becomes a social goal to be pursued within the norms set by *dharma*. And the *dhārmika* norms are set with an eye both on individual and social well-being. *Dharma* is the very basis of society and so whatever norms *dharma* lays down are always in keeping with social harmony and well-being. Similarly, *artha* is not a personal goal, because it is also to be pursued under the norms set by *dharma*. While accumulating things for material well-being, one is always to keep in mind that he is not trespassing upon the rights and properties of others, that he is not accumulating *artha* beyond a limit detrimental to the interests or well-being of other members of the society. And *dharma* by itself is definitely a social goal, firstly, because it regulates the functioning of *kāma* and *artha* and secondly, because all its principles are meant for individual virtues and duties in relation to other members of the society. Even where principles of *dharma* are principles of individual or personal morality, they are to have their impacts upon other members of the society.

All these are social goals in this simple sense also that they are all realisable within a society. These three, therefore—*kārma*, *artha* and *dharma*—form a cohesive trio in which *dharma* seems to be superior to both *kāma* and *artha*. *Mokṣa* by its special nature seems to be externally imposed. It has been added perhaps to act as a motivation for *dharma*. *Mokṣa* is regarded as having a special kind of ontological status and as such it is a metaphysical, trans-social goal for which all social, *dhārmika* activities somehow or other serve as means. It is as a matter of fact the case also that originally only three former *puruṣārthas*, known as *trivarga*, were recognised by Indian thinkers. This is accepted by almost all Indological scholars. The fourth *puruṣārtha*, giving place to *caturvarga* instead of *trivarga*, was added at some later stage of history. Again, a majority of Indian scholars favours the opinion that the *caturvarga* scheme of *puruṣārthas* is superior to the *trivarga* scheme in as much as the former removes the incompleteness of the latter and makes it more meaningful. It may be an important task for us as students of philosophy to see which one of the two is philosophically more sound and ethically more elevated. The latter task is rather more important for us here.

It seems undoubted that the *trivarga* scheme is at least ethically more elevated and sound. In this scheme naturally *dharma* finds the highest place by supervening over *kāma* and *artha*. A life in accordance with *dharma* in Indian setting is basically a life of morality. So in the *trivarga* scheme, morality is given the highest place. As human beings we have to perform certain duties and inculcate certain virtues. If these virtues, duties and obligations are taken as intrinsically valuable and not as means for some ulterior end, then a life of morality becomes valuable for its own sake. All the normal desires also are to be fulfilled according to the norms of morality. In Indian tradition itself systems like Prabhākara Mīmāṃsā advocate the intrinsic value-status of *dharma*. Even the *Bhagavadgītā* by its doctrine of *niṣkāma karma* or duty for duty sake advocates, in a way, the supremacy of *dharma*, although it does not seem to hold the *trivarga* theory of *puruṣārthas*. In any case, the *Bhagavadgītā* does not necessarily insist upon the performance of duty with an eye on *Mokṣa*. According to it, *Mokṣa* is the automatic result of *niṣkāma karma*. This seems to be the import of the following verses of the *Gītā*:

> "*Vihāya kāmān yaḥ sarvān, pumāṃścarati niḥspṛhaḥ*
> *nirmamo nirahaṃkāraḥ sa śāntimadhigacchati.*"[19]
> ("He who abandons all desires and acts free from longing, without any sense of mineness or egotism, he attains to peace.")

> "*tasmād asaktaḥ satataṃ kāryaṃ karma samācara*
> *asakto hy ācarana karma, param āpnoti pūruṣaḥ*".[20]
> ("Therefore, without attachment, perform always the work that has to be done, for man attains to the highest by doing work without attachment.")

For man to do the assigned duty (*svadharma*) is the highest value, *Mokṣa* is the spontaneous result of doing such a duty. So *Mokṣa* as a motivation is there, but it is not to be brought in as an aim while performing the duty. However, according to the *Bhagavadgītā*, if one works with the aim of *Mokṣa*, it will not be ordinarily regarded as an attached action. We cannot say that Gītā's doctrine of *niṣkāma karma* does not believe in *caturvarga* or does not take *Mokṣa* as the highest *puruṣārtha*. Although *Mokṣa* as *puruṣārtha* has not been discarded in the *Gītā* doctrine of *niṣkāma karma*, *dharma* has been given the highest place insofar as man's pursuit is concerned. He is to pursue his *dharma* as a thing of highest value, all else will follow on their own. So the spirit of taking *dharma* as the highest of human pursuits is in one sense there in the *Bhagavadgītā*.

Those who think that the addition of *Mokṣa* in the list of *puruṣārthas* makes the list complete are guided by the idea that *dharma* might not be resorted to without the motivation of *Mokṣa*. This is why they take *dharma* as a means to *Mokṣa*. The Vaiśeṣika sūtras, for example, define *dharma* as that which leads to *abhyudaya* and *niḥśreyasa*. Perhaps *Mokṣa* is taken as a motivation for *dharma* in the sense that without it people may not have a real incentive for the pursuit of *dharma*, but basically it seems to be a mistaken idea. After all, why is *Mokṣa* to be added as an incentive for *dharma*? Firstly, it is presumed that *dharma* by itself does not have enough inherent properties to attract people to pursue it for its own sake. Secondly, *Mokṣa* is more attractive and desirable as a goal and hence superior to *dharma*. But both these presuppositions seem to be ill-founded.

If for the pursuit of *dharma* the incentive of *Mokṣa* is assumed to be necessary, morality is reduced to prudence. If *dharma* is to be followed to gain personal advantage, this is a degradation of morality. We believe that *dahrma* requires no incentive other than itself. If men are made to understand properly that they have to act and behave as men, they may very well pursue *dharma* for its own sake. If men follow *dharma* for its own sake taking it as their bounden duty, morality will be accorded its due significance and status. The second assumption also does not stand on scrutiny. *Mokṣa* is, amongst other things, a status in which man is reduced to an eternal passivity. A life of suffering mixed with pleasure is life of activity and dynamism which has its own charm. A status of eternal calm may not be attractive for everybody. It may be a life of boredom. Moreover, how can it be assumed that even in terms of happiness a genuine *dhārmika* life is less happy than one which is attained after *Mokṣa*? We find that on many occasions people feel a real pleasure by helping others, by working for others. Why not may it be assumed that a man leading a real *dhārmika* life may derive immense happiness by discharging sincerely his moral obligations? This happiness will not be of a lower kind than the pure, elevated state of happiness. So, it cannot be said on any sound reasoning that the state of being after *Mokṣa* is qualitatively superior to a purely *dhārmika* life. That *Mokṣa* is superior to *dharma* may well be assumed, but it may not appear to be true for everybody. *Mokṣa* presents no justification for *dharma*, because no logical relation exists between the two.

Seen from a different angle, it may appear that because of giving *Mokṣa* the highest status and *dharma* a subsidiary place under the *caturvarga* theory of *puruṣārthas* a degradation of (moral) values has occurred. This is a matter of serious concern. *Mokṣa*, an elusive ideal, can hardly keep the common man attracted to it for long. Because *dharma* is regarded only a means to such an elusive ideal, it loses its real significance for the common man. The result is degradation of moral values. Had *dahrma* or morality been given the highest or intrinsic value-status, as is the position under the *trivarga* scheme, morality would perhaps have maintained its status and people would have always a genuine regard for the moral values. It is by adding *Mokṣa* to the *trivarga* scheme that the status of morality has been lowered. So the result has been counter-productive. Instead of giving morality a real significance, the addition of *Mokṣa* has really given place to a crisis of moral values. Hence, at least ethically speaking, the *trivarga* theory is superior to the *caturvarga* theory.

It may be seen from the above that if the theory of *puruṣārthas* is understood as the *trivarga* theory, it assumes great moral significance. It really serves as the psycho-moral foundation of the whole scheme of *sādhāraṇa* and *varṇāśrama dharmas*. The whole worldly life of man becomes a *dhārmika* or moral life. As even the pursuits of *kāma* and *artha* (which are the two major pursuits of worldly life) are to be effected under the yoke of *dharma*, the whole human life becomes a *dhārmika* life. As every scheme of individual or social life is formulated under the influence of the prevailing social realities, so the scheme of *puruṣārthas* also must have been formulated under the influence of the social realities prevailing in what may be called the classical Indian society.

The prevailing social realities that might have formed the background of the formulation of the theory of *puruṣārthas* include, rather pre-eminently, the division of individual's life into four stages (*āśrama vyavasthā*) and of the social life into four classes (*varṇa vyavasthā*). But apart from any such background also, the *trivarga* theory may be seen to work very effectively for any human society whatsoever, if at all that society consists of rational human beings. The *trivarga* theory really sets out a complete life plan for any individual who lives in a society. Any rational human being living in a society ought to aim at the three *puruṣārthas* conjointly and not alternatively.

6. Freedom and Responsibility

Ethical goodness consists in doing certain acts and refraining from certain others. But has man the option to do so? Has he the choice of opting for the right and refraining from the wrong or evil? This is a very important problem of ethics. If the problem is answered in the negative, the whole edifice of ethics will collapse. If man has no option, no choice, no freedom to choose between alternative courses of action, then it is meaningless to exhort him to do this and not to do that. Kant's maxim

'Thou oughtest, therefore thou can'st' is universally true, because to advise anybody to do one sort of thing in preference to the other has any meaning only when it is within his power to do what he wills to do. If everything is within the control of certain external, unseen forces and man is simply helpless to avoid such forces, all moral codes and counsels are useless. Now, what is the position in the Indian tradition in this regard? Before answering this question, however, we will have to be clear about what the freedom of man means in this context, i.e., what actually is meant by saying that he has a choice to opt between the right and the wrong.

The belief runs through the Indian tradition that under illusion or *avidyā* man is the slave of passions. This is the state of bondage, so there is no question of man being free. He will attain freedom only when he is able to break off the shackles of *avidyā*, i.e., by the attainment of true knowledge, *Jñāna*. What happens then to the counsel of making moral effort or of observing the *dharma?* Moral effort is not able to cause liberation, but it paves the way for higher spiritual effort. But man is not free at all, how then can he improve his lot by making moral effort? The real question is whether man has in any sense any option in his present state of *avidyā* to exercise his choice for the good and the right. The answer should obviously be in the affirmative in the Indian context, because otherwise the whole host of injunctions and prohibitions of the Śāstras will be meaningless. If man has no capacity, no power to opt between *dharma* and *adharma,* then how can it be legitimately expected of him to follow *dharma* and avoid *adharma*? How can he be held responsible and punished for any evil done by him? We have seen the law of *karma* envisaging that a man gets only what he deserves in virtue of the acts performed by him, but what will the word 'deserve' mean if man has no power to make his own choice and also to act according to his own choice? So, it seems in the light of the law of *karma* that man must be free in the choice of his actions. But the matter is not so easy and the law of *karma* itself generates complications in our coming to the conclusion straightway that man is free in his choice of actions. Let us see.

We have seen that the law of *karma* is the law of causation in the moral realm. The law of causation, we know, is deterministic. So, if the moral world is strictly governed by the law of *karma,* where is the scope for choice? Our present *karmas* are the natural corollary of our past *karmas.* Whatever we are in our present life is the result of what we had worked for in the past life. These potencies and dispositions which we have inherited from our past life actually determine our course of action in the present life. So there is no scope for free choice.

The real meaning of human freedom requires to be clearly understood. Determinism as a theory is understood to be opposed to human freedom, and therefore wherever there is determinism there can be no question of freedom. The point has been debated much in recent times and without going into the details of the debate it may safely be asserted that it is not determinism but indeterminism (which leaves everything to chance or fate), which is the real enemy of human freedom. Freedom is not the lack of all kinds of determinism. Freedom is hampered only if our will or action is determined by forces beyond our control; it is not hampered when it is determined by our own motives, desires, character etc. So freedom is not indeterminism, it is self-determinism. And the law of *karma* envisages nothing other than the doctrine of self-determinism. Whatever we are, it is due to our own *karmas* and whatever we will be, it will be on account of our own *karmas*. So, there is complete self-determinism in the moral realm. Nothing is left to chance or caprice of anybody under the working of the law of *karma*.

Under it there is always a scope to strive for the better, because as Dr. Radhakrishnan very ably says, "Life is like the game of bridge. The cards in the game are given to us. We do not select them. They are traced to past *karma* but we are free to make any call we think fit and lead any suit. Only we are limited by the rules of the game. We are more free when we start the game than later on when the game has developed and our choices become restricted. But till the very end there is always a choice."[21] So the law of *karma* does not mar man's freedom of making choice. Notwithstanding the determinism that the law envisages, there is scope for making correct choices for bettering our future. And above all, the kind of determinism that the law of *karma* enforces is nothing other than self-determinism, a determinism which is effected by our own past *karmas*.

So far we have seen that freedom of choice exists in the scheme of life in which the law of *karma* is an inevitable force. As the law of *karma* is the very presupposition of Indian ethics, there is clear scope for freedom in Indian ethics. In Indian moral thought it is perfectly meaningful to say that a person is himself responsible for the good or bad consequences that he has to undergo because of his good or bad actions. In short, in Indian view of life the law of *karma* is the backbone of any talk of morality. But let us now see the actual position in this regard with reference to the various texts and systems of Indian thought. The logical scope for freedom is there, but what do the texts and systems actually hold in this respect?

We have seen that determinism is not the real enemy of freedom. That all our actions have their causes is not to rule out freedom of choice, specially when we ourselves—our own motives and dispositions—are the causes of our actions. The real enemy of freedom is indeterminism or fatalism or providence or whatever other name we give to the unseen force beyond our control. If we refer to Indian texts, we may find that the role of fate or providence, generally known as *daiva*, has been so often recognised in determining our course of actions. The *Artharva Veda*, for example, gives all casual power to what is called *kāla* (time or destiny).[22] In the *Rāmāyaṇa* there are various spots where fate or destiny has been given the supreme status. When Rāma hears about banishment due to Kaikeyī's boon, he does not in the least blame Kaikeyī. He rather praises her for her sweet and kind heart and attributes everything to destiny: Similarly, when Sītā is disowned and banished by Rāma due to the raising of public eyebrows on her purity, she blames nobody and attributes everything to her fate.

As a matter of fact, in the ancient Hindu literature the unsurpassable power of fate is generally recognised. The fate or destiny however has more often been taken as pre-ordained by God. "There is one ordainer and no second .... Controlled by the great ordainer, I go on as He sets me on, like water along a downward path. . . Doing acts that tend towards the direction of virtue, and also those tend towards the opposite direction, I go on as he sets me on. One gets those things that are ordained to be got. That which is to happen actually happens. One has to reside repeatedly in such wombs in which one is placed by the ordainer. One has no choice in the matter."[23] The passage clearly exposes the undauntable power of destiny over man, although the overall power lies only in the hands of God. But God is never assumed to be acting whimsically or arbitrarily in deciding the fate of a man once for all. He is rather guided in this work by the actions done by the person in his past career.

As it is said in the *Mahābhārata* itself, "The Supreme Lord and the ordainer of all or ordaineth everything in respect of the weal and woe, the happiness and misery, of all creatures, even prior to their births, guided by the acts of each, which are even like a seed, O hero amongst men, as a wooden doll is made to move its limbs by the wire-puller, so are creatures made to work by the Lord of all. . . . . .Like a bird tied with a string every creature is dependent on God. . . . No one can be his own ordainer. Like a pearl on its string, or a bull held fast by the cord passing through its nose, or a tree fallen from the bank into the middle of the stream, every creature followeth the command of the creator. . . ."[24] The hard note of irreprehensible destiny is very loudly audible here, but while framing the chain of destiny the Lord is said to have taken into consideration the past deeds of man. So the destiny works very much in the frame of the law of *karma*.

Yet, human effort is critically important and that man has freedom to act, if only he has the will to do so. As a matter of fact, destiny (*Daiva*) and human effort (*Puruṣakāra*) are the two wheels of the same cart. "As there can be no movement of a cart with (only) one wheel, (even) so *Daivam* does not succeed without human effort."[25] Again "He that lieth at ease without activity, believing in destiny alone, is soon destroyed like an unburnt earthen pot in water. So also he that believeth in chance and sitteth inactive though capable of activity, liveth not long, for his life is one of weakness and helplessness. For all this, however, a person should act."[26] Destiny is made up, for the most part, of one's own past deeds. So ultimately it is one's own activities which count. How can then destiny mean or allow inaction?

Our previous actions themselves form our destiny. Therefore our present will make our future. The significance of our efforts lies in properly understanding the meaning of destiny itself. "The success of a work lies in destiny and efforts; of them efforts of a pristine birth are manifested in destiny."[27] Buch very ably says in this respect, "Fate is the capital, while our present *karma* is the income. If we merely centre our attention on enjoyment, our capital will be gradually lost. Fresh efforts are necessary to add to the capital of our good deeds. It is here that the usefulness of our own efforts, our *puruṣārtha,* lies. We are governed by the past; but we can govern the future, because our present deeds will be crystallised into destiny."[28]

On a proper understanding of the meaning of *Daiva,* human effort does not in any way prove to be irrelevant. It is rather necessary because one's destiny itself is a result for the most part of his own deeds. And clearly enough where there is scope for effort, the role of freedom or choice is also there. If one's effort means something, then he must have his own choice in making that effort, because otherwise personal effort will not have any real sense. The *Mahābhārata* recognises it when it asserts, "Man, having first settled some purpose in his mind, accomplisheth it himself working with the aid of his intelligence. We, therefore, say that man himself is the cause (of what he doeth) . . . . . If a person were not, in the matter of his acts, himself the cause thereof, then sacrifices would not bear any fruits in his case, nor would anybody be a disciple or a master. It is because a person is himself the cause of his work that he is applauded when he achieveth success, and censured if he fails. If a man were not the cause of his acts, how would all this be justified?"[29]

So, the significance of human effort and consequently that of man's freedom to choose are to be accepted as facts, because otherwise rewards and punishments, applause and censure for one 's acts become meaningless. Śaṃkara also realises the importance of human freedom to make personal efforts, because otherwise moral life will have no meaning and the teaching of the Śāstras will be purposeless.[30] The Mīmāṃsakas also seem to take a similar view when they point out that it would be a moral as well as logical absurdity to take the *Vidhi* as an imperative upon the (moral) agent on the one hand and then deny the power of freedom to the agent for accomplishing it on thte other. The imperative of the *Vidhi* implies the agent's capability to accomplish it because the *Vidhi* is *Pravartanārūpa.* As the *Śāstradīpikā* says:

> *"pravartanā rūpo hi Vidhiḥ arthāt samīhitasādhana-*
> *śaktim bodhayati-pravartanā ca aśakyaviṣaye na sambhavati"* [31]

There cannot, thus, be any moral injunction which the agent is not free to accomplish.

So, according to the Indian view, man has got freedom to choose and to act; he is the cause of his own actions, so that a responsible moral life may have meaning. But we must understand here what his freedom actually means. He is not free in the sense that his actions are completely undetermined and arbitrary. On the other hand, rather, he is determined in his choice of actions by his own dispositions, his own habit and his own character, which are all determined to a great extent by his own past *karmas.* So he is determined in his choice all the same, but the determination does not come from any power or agency other than himself. It is therefore self-determination and consequently freedom. Being determined by one's own character and habits cannot be taken as being robbed of freedom of choice. In our life we are determined to a great extent in our choice of actions by our own habits and character. On that account we are not spared of the responsibility for our actions. For, it is realised that the habits and the character that are determining our actions now are after all the results of our own past choices and actions. We have freely chosen them to be the guiding principles of our actions. So even in spite of them we are taken as acting freely and consequently held responsible for our actions. Similarly, all our actions are determined by our own dispositions, character and habit formed as a consequence of actions done in the present or past life. Even what is called destiny is a result of our own past *karmas.* So the law of *karma* reigns supreme in the Indian view of life, but it is a repository of freedom in the sense of self-determination and not of complete determinism where there is no scope for freedom and choice.

There is one more point in the Indian view of freedom: the overall supremacy of God in determining human will and action. Here again human freedom seems to be in jeopardy. If God wields power to make a human being act in a way he does, where is the scope for man's freedom and responsibility? This problem is not of Indian philosophy alone. The Western philosophers and theologians also have always grappled with the problem equally. Śaṃkara tries to bring about the reconciliation in this connection in the following manner, "The Lord makes the soul act, having regard to the efforts made by it, whether meritorious or non-meritorious. . . .the Lord arranges favourable or unfavourable circumstances for the souls with a view to their former efforts. . . . . But if the activity of the soul is dependent on something else, this having regard (on the part of the Lord) to former effort is inappropriate.—By no means, we reply; for although the activity of the soul is not independent, yet the soul does not. The Lord indeed causes it to act, but it acts itself. Moreover, the Lord in causing it to act now has regard to its former efforts, and he caused it to act in a former existence, having regard to its efforts previous to that existence, a *regressus*, against which, considering the eternity of the *saṃsāra*, no objections can be reaised.—But how is it known that the Lord has regard to efforts made (in former existences)?—The Sūtra replies: from the purportlessness etc. of injunctions and prohibitions."[32]

It may be seen that the basis of reconciliation here is again the law of *karma*. God, the Lord, is no doubt, supreme and in a sense it is he who is the cause of every action, because everyone who acts is caused to act by him, but God does not act arbitrarily. He takes into consideration the former acts done by a person and accordingly arranges the situation for his further activities. In spite of his all-powerfulness God allows freedom to people in matters of their actions. The omnipotent God does not transgress the law of *karma*. It is argued that all the injunctions and prohibitions, do's and don't's of the Vedas (attributed to God Himself) would be meaningless if God would not grant people freedom to act in terms of their past *karmas*. For the injunctions and prohibitions to have some real significance, human effort must be given due importance.

Rāmānuja also takes up the problem of human freedom and, like Śaṃkara, tries to give human effort its due significance without robbing God of his omnipotence. He however understands the whole situation in his own way. He realises the necessity of freedom granted to human beings to act. But he is not ready to accept that man has absolute freedom. The overall lordship of God is maintained and man is allowed only a limited kind of freedom. Nevertheless, this freedom is of a kind which fully makes room for man himself being held responsible for his deeds. Rāmānuja says that no action is possible without God's permission. But such permission may be secured by man's own genuine efforts. If a man is habitually disposed to do good acts, God engenders in his mind a tendency to do virtuous actions while he who seems habitually disposed to bad actions is driven by God to perform evil actions under such situations. Although God causes men to act, he makes them act in accordance with their own efforts, dispositions and habits. Even the permission that one has to seek from God is for the most part a thing of his own making. In this respect, God treats men as his partner. A partner willing to transfer a joint property to a third party has to take permission from the other partner. Similarly, it is the responsibility of man to secure permission from God and for that he will have to make himself worthy by his efforts. Good efforts draw inspiration from God for good works, while efforts in the bad direction draw inspiration from God for bad actions. Because God respects man's own efforts, own dispositions etc., which, perhaps, he has inherited from his past deeds, so God has granted limited freedom to man and insofar as man is free, he is responsible for his good or bad actions.

In this sense the injunctions and prohibitions of the Śāstras do not prove to be meaningless. While commenting on the Sūtra II.3.41 of the Brahmasūtras Rāmānuja's own words are as follows: "The inwardly ruling highest self promotes action insofar as it regards in the case of any action the volitional effort made by the individual soul, and then adds that effort by granting its favour or permission (*anumati*); action is not possible without permission on the part of the higest self. In this way (i.e. since the action primarily depends upon the volitional effort of the soul) injunctions and prohibitions are not devoid of meaning. . . The case is analogous to that of property of which two men are joint owners. If one of these wishes to transfer that property to a third person, he cannot do so without permission of the partner but that permission is given is after all his own doing, and hence the fruit of the action (reward or anything) properly belongs to him only. . . . the Lord wishing to do a favour to those who are resolved on acting so as fully to please the highest person, engenders in their minds a tendency towards highly virtuous actions, while on the other hand, in order to punish those who are resolved on lines of actions altogether displeasing to him, he engenders in their minds a delight in such actions as have a downward tendency and are obstacles in the way of the attainment of the Lord." God has the ultimate power to make man act; the latter paves the way for his action himself and to that extent he is free and responsible.

Indian moral tradition gives ample room to human freedom without which various injunctions and prohibitions of the Śāstras would have been logically unacceptable. However, the freedom is essentially tied up with the law of *karma*. The law, no doubt, brings in a kind of determinism, but because that determinism is self-determinism, it is really freedom. One is determined in his present actions by the dispositions and tendencies earned by him due to his own past *karmas*, and therefore in doing whatever he does he has freedom in the real moral sense. In this chain of self-determination, there is ample scope for fresh human effort and endeavour so as to change his future lot. Even God and destiny who seem to bind the individual in a chain of helplessness do not work in defiance of the *karmas* performed by the individual in his past life. Destiny is the other name for the capital that one has stored by virtue of his past deeds. And God also wields his power to get the man act always giving due consideration to the deeds done by him in his past life.

7. *Rāga* (Affection or Attachment) and *Dveṣa* (Aversion)

According to Nyāya, our actions originate from three sources: (1) *Doṣa* (2) *Saṃkalpa* and (3) *Prayojana*. The term '*doṣa*' denotes individual's primary or basic disposition towards objects and (by extension) all the feelings that are stirred up by them. A *saṃkalpa* is a mental predisposition that arises from the recollection of objects that have been previously experienced.[33] They consist in mental moods that are felt as delightful, hateful or confusing according to the tone of the remembered experience. As the predispositions are induced by recollections, their emergence into consciousness is conditioned by the factors that prompt recollection. *Prayojana*, sometimes translated as 'motive', is "that about which the decision (to acquire it or to shun it) having been taken one sets to act".[34] Thus *prayojana* or motive is the object, aiming either to have or to reject which one resorts to action.[35] The primary motive, however, according to Vātsyāyana is pleasure for which either the object is desired to be achieved or shunned.

Doṣa is divided into three groups: (1) *Rāga*, (2) *Dveṣa*, and (3) *Moha*.[36] It is these *doṣas* which are regarded as the direct sources of action. This is why '*doṣa*' is defined in the Nyāya Sūtras as that which causes activity (*pravarttanā lakṣaṇā doṣāḥ*).[37] But in a sense, the *saṃkalpas* (predispositions) precede the *doṣas* (dispositions), because when the former mature into the latter, actions take place.[38] Of the three *doṣas*, again, *moha* is the worst, because it is under the impact of *moha* (delusion) that *rāga* and *dveṣa* arise (*teṣāṃ mohaḥ pāpīyānnāmūḍhasyetarot patte*).[39] Thus in a way, *moha* becomes the most basic of the three *doṣas*, because it is out of *moha* that *rāga* and *dveṣa* arise. Had there been no *moha*, *rāga* and *dveṣa* could not have come about at all, and consequently there would have been no action.

Moha is delusion or wrong apprehension and judgement. *Rāga* is attachment with or affection for an object whereas *dveṣa* is aversion or repulsion from it. We have generally attraction for or attachment with an object which we feel on the basis of our past experience as giving us pleasure. So *rāga* is nothing but attachment with favourable object (*anukūla viṣayeṣurāgaḥ*). Similarly, we have repulsion from object which we feel on the basis of our past experience as giving us pain. So *dveṣa* is repulsion from the unfavourable object (*pratikūla viṣayeṣu dveṣaḥ*). *Rāga* and *dveṣa* are therefore regarded as the springs of our action. It is for the attainment of pleasure and avoidance of pain that we act. The object of *rāga* or *dveṣa* forms the immediate motive for which we act. Thus motive is a moment in the process of activity generated by *rāga* and *dveṣa*.

The following are the different kinds of *rāga* (attachment) according to Nyāya: *kāma* (lust), *spṛhā* (avarice), *tṛṣṇā* (avidity) and *lobha* (covetousness). *Kāma* is lust or craving for any sensuous pleasure including the pleasure of sex. *Spṛhā* is the desire for worldly possessions. *Tṛṣṇā* is the desire to live and live so as to cling to worldly objects. *Lobha* is the desire for getting forbidden things.

The following are the different kinds of *dveṣa*: *krodha* (anger), *īrṣyā* (enevy), *asūyā* (jealousy), *droha* (malevolence) and *amarṣa* (malice). *Krodha* is the emotional flare up with the loss of rational balance. It is a kind of aversion because it occurs in face of an object, person or situation which we do not like and which therefore disturbs our rational balance. *Īrṣyā* is unbearability regarding the prosperity of others. Jealousy is unbearability regarding good or appreciable qualities in others. *Droha* or malevolence is the tendencey to do harm to others. *Amarṣa* is implicit desire for revenge.

Moha (delusion) has been classified into *mithyājñāna* (misapprehension), *vicikitsā* (suspicion), *māna* (arrogance or vanity) and *pramāda* (carelessness of lack of earnestness).

It is to be mentioned in this connection that the Vaiśeṣikas take *icchā* (desire) and *dveṣa* (aversion) as the basic springs of action and *rāga* is taken by them as one of the kinds of desire. They interpret *icchā* or desire in the following manner:

Icchā consists in the wishing for something not already obtained, either for one's own sake or for the sake of other. (Thus desire can be either egoistic or altruistic.) It proceeds from the contact of the mind and soul through pleasure etc. or through remembrance. It is the source of effort, virtues and vice. *Kāma* (lust), *abhilāṣā* (hunger), *rāga* (affection or attachment), *saṃkalpa* (aspiration), *kāruṇya* (compassion), *vairāgya* (dispassion or disinclination), *upadhā* (disposition to deceive), *bhava* (concealed desire) and so on are some of the forms of desire. Lust is desire for sensuous (including sexual) enjoyment. Hunger is desire for food. Affection is the desire for repeated experiencing of the object. Aspiration is the desire for bringing about something not near at hand. Compassion is the desire for the removal of others' trouble. Dispassion or disinclination is the desire for renouncing an object after finding something wrong with it. Disposition to deceive is the desire for deceiving others. Concealed desire is unexpressed desire.[40] So, these are the various kinds of desire which prompt action. It can be seen that *rāga* has been taken here as a kind of desire and has been interpreted as the desire to cling to an object so as to repeatedly experience or enjoy it. *Rāga* is thus very intense desire.

Dveṣa has been interpreted by Praśastapāda in the following manner: It is of the nature of heart-burning or irritation. It is the feeling that makes one think himself burning or being irritated (*dveṣaḥ prajvalānatmakaḥ*). It proceeds from the contact of the soul with the mind aided either by pain or by remembrance of pain. *Krodha* (anger), *droha* (revengefulness), *manyu* (concealed ill-will), *akṣamā* (jealousy) and *amarṣa* (envy) are the various forms of *dveṣa*. *Krodha* is that aversion which produces certain physical changes in the body and quickly disappears. It causes violent tremor and agitation. *Droha* is not perceptible by any outward sign. It is deep-seated inclination of revenge resulting in harm which lingers for some time. *Manyu* is concealed ill will. It is the aversion that lies hidden in the mind due to the man not being able to retaliate upon the person who might have harmed him. *Akṣamā* is the feeling of aversion against the presence of good qualities in some other person. *Amarṣa* is the feeling of aversion arising from the fact of one's own good points being surpassed by those of other people.[41]

8. *Kleśa*

The word ordinarily means pain or trouble, but in the Indian tradition, specially in the Buddhist tradition, it has been used in a technical sense to signify passions which defile or corrupt. The equivalent Pāli term is '*kileśo*'. According to the Buddhist literature, it is this which is the root of all sinful actions which bind. The Pāli Piṭakas enumerate the following ten *kleśas—lobho* (greed), *doṣo* (hatred), *moho* (delusion), *māno* (pride), *ditathi* (heretical view), *vicikicchā* (doubt), *thīnam* (sloth), *uddhaccam* (arrogance), *ahirikā* (shamelessness), *anottapyam* (recklessness). The Buddhist Sanskrit literature enumerates six *kleśas*[42] and twenty-four *upakleśas.*[43]

In the Nyāya system the word '*kleśa*' has been used both in the sense of pain and passion. When in the *Nyāya Sūtra* (of Gautamā) it is said that '*suṣuptasya svapnādarśane kleśābhāvavadapavargaḥ*'[44] the word '*kleśa*' is used in the sense of pain or suffering, but when the same word is used again as saying '*na pravṛttiḥ pratisandhānāya hīnakleśasya*'[45] here it (the word '*kleśa*') is used in the sense of passions which bind. It is said here that for those whose *kleśas* have been destroyed, no action is productive of effects. Here it seems the word '*kleśa*' has been used more or less in the sense of '*doṣa*'.

Similarly, while it is said in the Vaiśeṣika system that when *kleśas* like ignorance, egoism, affection, aversion etc. are destroyed, the actions being like unhusked rice cease to produce merit and demerit,[46] then clearly the word '*kleśa*' has been used in the sense of defiling passions which generate attached actions and consequently produce binding effects.

9. *Aicchika* and *Anaicchika Karmas* (Voluntary and Non-Voluntary Actions)

We know that the distinction between voluntary and non-voluntary actions is important for ethics, because it is only the former which constitute the proper subject-matter of ethics. This important distinction between two kinds of actions was recognised in Indian thought in as early a period as that of Praśastapāda, who in his commentary on the Vaiśeṣika philosophy brought about a clear distinction between the non-voluntary and voluntary actions *Jīvanapūrvaka prayatna* and *Icchādveṣapūrvaka prayatna.*

Prayatna (effort or activity), says Praśastapāda, may be of two kinds: One proceeds from mere living and the other from desire and aversion. The former carries on the upward and downward breathings in the sleeping man and at the state of awakening brings about the contact of the mind with the various organs of perception. This effort is the direct result of the contact of the soul and mind aided by *dharma* and *adharma* (merit and demerit). The second kind of effort centres around activities leading to the retaining of desirable and abandoning of the undesirable object; and it also conduces to actions calculated to keep the body in a state of steady equilibrium; this effort proceeds from the contact of the soul and mind, aided by desires and aversions.[47]

The former kind of automatic or reflex actions occur without any conscious will on the part of the doer. These actions are done by virtue of the simple fact that the doer is a living being. In other words, they follow spontaneously from his biological nature. The other kind of actions, however, are done with conscious will for the fulfilment of specific purpose—the attainment of pleasure and avoidance of pain. Such actions have another purpose also and that is the maintenance of the equilibrium of the body. This shows that according to Praśastapāda voluntary actions are purposive. There is, of course, a purpose behind the automatic or reflex actions also, but that purpose is not consciously aimed at. In case of voluntary actions, however, the purpose is consciously aimed at. So the essential character of voluntary action is conscious aiming and choice.

The neo-Naiyāyikas also distinguish between voluntary and non-voluntary actions and make the distinction rather more explicit and clear by adding *svecchādhinatva* as a necessary condition of voluntary actions. *Svecchādhinatva* implies an action being within one's own free choice. So, according to this view, voluntary actions besides being the results of conscious choice are also the results of one's own free will. Voluntary actions in this respect are different not only from the reflex actions of the organism (*jīvanpūrvaka prayatna*) but also from all actions prompted by blind impulses.

10. *Śreyaḥ* and *Preyaḥ* (The Good and the Pleasant)

As early as in the Upaniṣads, a very important ethically significant distinction was made between the good and the pleasant, the desirable and the desired, in the form of the distinction between *śreyaḥ* and *preyaḥ*. The *Kaṭhopaniṣad* says in this connection: "The *Śreyaḥ* is one thing and the *Preyaḥ* is another. They attract the individual in different ways to different objects or ends. He who chooses *Śreyaḥ* rises higher but he who chooses the *Preyaḥ* fails in his aim." (*anyacchreyo'nyadutaiva preyaste ubhe nānārthe puruṣaṃ sīnītaḥ. tayoḥ śreyādadānasya sādhu bhavati hīyate'rthād yaḥ preyo vṛṇite.*)[48]

A clear distinction has been made between (the ethically or spiritually) higher pursuits of life and the mere pleasurable ends. One who pursues the former does the right thing and one who follows the path of mere pleasurable experiences fails in his mission. Man is not to be guided by mere passions, or by his natural inclinations. He is rather to be guided by the higher faculties of his life, such as, reason, conscience etc., which will instruct or guide him to achieve that end and orient him towards higher spiritual pursuits. Śaṃkara takes '*śreyaḥ*' to mean *niḥśreyasa* or the highest good, the *summum bonum.* So according to him the path of *śreyaḥ* is the path of the highest good, whereas the path of *preyaḥ* is the path of mere empirical pleasure which generates bondage. *Preyaḥ* is what is usually desired but the desired is not the desirable too. The desirable is something else. Man should control his passions for worldly pleasure and orient himself towards the desirable; he should pass from 'is' to 'ought'. The essence of morality really lies in briddling the lower passions, the natural bodily inclinations so as to adopt and cultivate the higher, the spiritual and the moral.

The good and the pleasant, the desirable and the desired, come in mixed forms. But man is to discriminate between the higher and the lower, and adopt the former and shun the latter. The wise man does this while the ignorant does the opposite. The *Kaṭhopaniṣad,* therefore, says furthermore: "The *Śreyaḥ* and the *Preyaḥ* come up to man mixed up together. The wise man discriminates and then chooses the former (the course of virtue) and rejects the latter (the course of worldly pleasure). The foolish man, on the other hand, chooses the pleasurable, the *Preyaḥ.*" (*śreyaśca preyaśca manusyametastau samparītya vivinakti dhīraḥ. śreyohi dhīraḥ abhipreyaso vṛṇīte preyo mando yogakṣemād vṛṇīte*).[49]

In the above Upaniṣadic distinction (between *preyaḥ* and *śreyaḥ*), therefore, lies the seed of the early Indian moral consciousness. The ultimate according to Indian thought, is, spiritual end, the *Mokṣa,* to which *śreyaḥ* refers. But the distinction arouses a moral consciousness in man. It cautions to the effect that man's aim is not simply to enjoy things of wordly life, to fulfil narrow interests. His real mission is to rise higher, during the course of which he is prove to live a life of higher pursuits, a life of certain moral virtues which will ultimately lead to the spiritual fulfilment. Regulation and control of the basic instincts and adoption of altruistic ends naturally come up as his legitimate pursuit the moment he understands the distinction between what he desires and what is desirable for him. Adoption of good and desirable pursuits brings him on a path suitable to carry on his life's journey to reach for fulfilment.

REFERENCES

1. *RV* X.190.1.
2. *Ibid.*, IV.23.8-10.
3. *Ibid.*, IX.73.6.
4. *Ibid.*, X.124.5.
5. *Ibid.*, 1.152.1.
6. John Mckenzie, *op. cit.*, pp. 38-39.
7. K.V. Rangaswami Aiyangar, *Some Aspects of the Hindu View of Life According to Dharmaśāstra* (Baroda: Oriental Institute,1952), p. 63.
8. P.S. Sivaswamy Aiyer, *Evolution of Hindu Ethical Ideals*, Calcutta University Press, 1935), pp. 19-20.
9. *BG* II.35.
10. *Manu* VIII.15.
11. S. Radhakrishnan, *Indian Philosophy*, Vol. I, p. 245.
12. M. Hiriyanna, *Essentials of Indian Philsophy*, p. 48.
13. *BG* III.25.
14. *Ibid.*, V.II.
15. *Ibid.*, II.47.
16. *Ibid.*, V.10.
17. *Ibid.*, III.30.
18. S. Radhakrishnan, *Eastern Religions* etc., p. 353.
19. *BG* II.71.
20. *Ibid.*, III.19.
21. S. Radhakrishnan, *An Idealist View of Life* (London, Allen and Unwin, 1932), p. 279.
22. *AV* XIX. 53-54.
23. The *Mahābhārata*, Śānti Parva, 233, 9-12.
24. *Ibid.*, Vana Parva, 30, 30-36.
25. *YV* 1.351.
26. The *Mahābhārata*, Vana Parva, 32, 27-29.
27. *YV* 1.349.
28. M.A. Buch, *The Principles of Hindu Ethics* (Hathi Pole, Baroda, 1921), p. 555.
29. *The Mahābhārata*, Vana Parva, 32.3, 20.
30. Śaṃkara's Commentary on *BG* III.33.
31. Quoted by S.K. Maitra in his *op. cit.*, p. 152.
32. *SB* II.3.43.
33. *NB* 3.1.26 (G.N. Jha's trans., *Gautama's Nyāya-Sūtras* (with *Vātsyāyana's Bhāṣya)*, Poona Oriental Series.
34. *Ibid.*, 1.124.
35. *Ibid.*, 1.1.1.
36. *NS* 4.1.3.
37. *NS* 1.1.18.
38. *NB* 4.1.68.
39. *NS* 4.1.6.
40. *Padārthadharmasaṃgraha* of Praśastapāda with the *Nyāya Kandali* of Śrīdhara, Tr. G.N. Jha, VI.II.10-14; 1.1.6.

41. *Ibid.*, VI.II.14, V.I.1, I.1.6.
42. *rāgaḥ pratigho māno'vidyā kudṛṣṭirvicikitsā ceti.*

—*Dharmasaṃgraha* LXVIII

43. *krodha upanāho mrakṣah pradāśa īrṣyām mātsaryam śāṭhyam māyā mado vihiṃsā hṛḥ anapatrapā styānamaśrāddhya kausīdya pramādo muṣitasmṛtirvikṣepo' samprajanyam kaukṛtyam middham vitardo'vicāraśceti.*

—*Dharmasaṃgraha* LXIX

44. *NS* 4.1.63.
45. *NS* 4.1.64.
46. *Padārthadharmasaṃgraha* with Śrīdhar's *Nyāya Kandali* VI.II, V.II.16.18.
47. *Padārthadharmasaṃgraha* VI, II.14, V.I.1, V.II.14.I.I.6.
48. *Kaṭha Up*. 2.1.
49. *Ibid.*, 2.2.

CHAPTER XI

Justification of Morality in Indian Thought

1. Question of Justification

Discussion in the preceding chapters shows that Indian society like other societies of the world has recognised from very old days the worth of the institution of morality. People have been advised to do certain things and refrain from certain others. Some acts are regarded virtuous, good, right etc., while others are regarded sinful, bad, wrong etc. Yet a rational man always reserves the right to ask, why he should perform particular acts and shun others. What might be the justification behind counsels of do's and don't's? If someone answers 'because it is the demand of morality to follow certain specific acts and refrain from others', the most fundamental question, 'why be moral at all?', or 'why to adopt the moral course of action?' can still be asked. Questions of justification may be of three levels: (1) of the level of particular acts, (2) of the level of particular principles or laws which govern such acts, (3) of the most fundamental level, i.e., of the level of the rationality of the institution of morality itself. In other words questions may be raised about (1) the judgements of moral obligation (such as, 'speak the truth', 'Do not steal', etc.), (2) the judgements of moral value (such as, 'stealing' is-wrong', 'keeping passions under control is good', etc.), (3) the institution of morality or the moral point of view itself (why be moral at all? or why adopt the moral point of view at all?).

Such questions have been very extensively raised and answered in the Western ethics, especially in the modern Western ethics, which goes mostly by the name of meta-ethics. Judgements concerning particular acts have been sought to be justified with reference to the related judgements of principles or laws under which the respective former judgements may be subsumed. Judgements of principles or laws in their turn have been sought to be justified with reference to principles of relatively higher generality, and so on. Opinions differ on the question, 'what will be the nature of such justifications in logical terms?' Justifications of all sorts, no doubt, take, in some sense or other, the forms of arguments in which the judgement of particular act or principle to be justified becomes the conclusion and the justifying principles form the premises.

While some take these arguments as merely pursuasive (Stevenson),[1] others regard them as perfectly deductive (Hare),[2] and still others take these deductive arguments as of some special forms, based not on the notion of strict logical implication, but on the notion of what is called 'contextual implication' (Nowell-Smith).[3] We are not going to elaborate here all these ideas, because that will lead us too far. What we want simply to point out that while conscious attempts have been elaborately made in the West to advance (rational) justification for our moral acts and principles, little efforts have been made by Indian moral thinkers in this regard. In fact, they never realised any need for advancing justificatory arguments for the moral precepts and principles. The reason is obvious. We have seen that the primary source of morality in India is authority. So, justification for any moral precept or principle is to be sought for in the authority. Justification of a moral act or principle is found in the citation of the Vedas or the Smṛtis or in the path set out or trod by great people or in the dictates of one's conscience. In other words, to the question why one should do a particular act in preference to the other or should follow a particular principle of action, the simple answer is: the Śāstras enjoin upon us to do so or the great sages have followed that path or the path is concurred by the voice of conscience. Harldy any reference to reason or logic is advised to be resorted to. In fact, resort to reasoning for justifying any action or principle in supersession to the scriptures has beeen regarded as heresy, blasphemy and something undesirable. If any role is assigned to reason, its exact nature has hardly been ever deciphered in clear terms.

The search for justification of morality leads us to the question, "why be moral at all?" To this question the Indian thinkers have remained all the more silent. They have possibly assumed that it is the inherent obligation of man to be moral besides everything else. Any doubt about the desirability or rationality of the institution of morality is unsacred, and is as good as doubting the authority, veracity etc. of the sacred texts like the Vedas. The Vedas, Smṛtis etc. enjoin upon us to do certain acts and desist from others. So, it is our duty to follow the dictates of these scriptures. The injuctions and prohibitions laid down in the Śāstras are meant to be followed, and therefore they are to be followed. The justification for being moral again comes from authority itself. If we do not adopt the moral point of view, we ignore and defy the Śāstras, which is an act of sacrilege.

2. Two Senses of Justification

Before saying anything about the Indian stand on the question, we would like to consider at some length what the question of justification itself implies. The question may either mean asking for a motivation or a rational justification for morality. When we ask 'why be moral at all?', the 'why?' of it may either be a demand for the motivation for morality or for a rational justification thereof. In the first sense, 'why?' will mean 'what for?'. So the question is, 'what for one should be moral, what is he going to gain by being moral?'. When Bradley raised the question of the justification of morality, he raised it in this first sense, i.e., in the sense of the motivation for morality. He opined that to make morality a means for some ulterior end was to degrade it. Morality must be its own end, its own justification.[4]

In the second sense, the question is asked by way of demanding the reason for being moral. Thus, in this sense, the question 'why should I be moral?' or 'why should I follow the prescriptions of *dharma*?' is equivalent to the question 'what is the reason which makes it obligatory upon me to follow the prescriptions of *dharma*?'.

But here the word 'reason' itself may be taken as ambiguous. Giving reason in one sense may mean advancing premise or set of premises out of which it may be deduced that the prescriptions of *dharma* (or morality) are to be followed. But in this sense, perhaps, justifying morality (as an institution) is an impossible task. Individual judgements or moral acts or principles 'may be justified in this manner (e.g. 'Do not steal' may be justified by 'Stealing is bad' or 'you ought to keep your promise' may be justified by 'All promises ought to be kept'), but justifying the whole institution of morality in this manner is not possible. For, what, after all, will be the premise or premises out of which it will follow that one is to observe morality or the prescriptions of *dharma?* Perhaps this is why the question 'why be moral?, as a justificatory question, has sometimes been regarded improper which cannot be answered. Even justifying individual moral acts or principles in the above manner has its necessary limit. In that process we have to go on and on backwards in search of moral principles of higher and higher generality. There will be a stage to reach for the ultimate justificatory principle, if we do not want to fall in infinite regress. As we know, thinkers like Hare and Nowell-Smith had to say that this ultimate justifying principles could only be a matter of personal decision.[5] Even having tied this decision hypothesis with the principle of universalizability,[6] Hare was not able to lift the ultimate justificatory principle to a really objective status. So, if we cannot justify the individual moral acts and principles to the end in a purely objective and rational sense, then what to talk of justifying the whole institution of morality or *dharma* in that manner?

In yet another sense 'giving reason' will mean adopting the rational course or the course of reasonableness. Here 'rational' does not mean logical or deductive, but simply reasonable or appealing to reason. Observing the death of a few persons like Ram, Shyam, Mohan etc. does not form a sufficient logical ground for any one to conclude that all men are mortal, because the latter does not follow deductively out of the former, but still it is reasonable to believe in the truth of the latter on the ground of the former. Similarly, when one counsels somebody not to smoke cigarettes and says by way of advancing reason for the same that 'because cigarette is injurious to health', he is not advancing reason in the strict logical sense because, the former does not deductively follow out of the latter, but still he is presenting a fairly reasonable ground before the person concerned to dissuade him from smoking cigarettes. Thus, there is a sense in which advancing rational ground or giving reason for something simply means presenting something as the ground which sounds reasonable or appealing to general human reason.

In this sense, the question 'why be moral?' may be answered, for instance, by saying: 'because morality (being moral) follows from the very nature of man'. Here it should be very much kept in mind that the word 'follows' does not mean 'logically or deductively follows'. Rather, it simply means that taking human nture as it is, it is quite rational or very much reasonable to assert that he is to adopt or ought to adopt the moral course. Here *dharma* or morality is to be observed not for some motive of attaining something nor for the fact that being moral deductively follows from some higher principle but simply for the fact that one's own specific nature forms a reason for one's being moral. If man is said to be an animal he is still distinct from all other animals by virtue of his rationality. Because of this unique feature which separates him from others certain specific way of conduct will be reasonably expected of him. If he does not behave the way he is expected to do, his conduct can be said to be not justified by his inherent nature.

3. Justification in Indian Thought

Now let us see the position in Indian ethical thought. The obvious answer to the question of justification in the first sense (i.e. in the sense of motivation) will be, 'For attaining *Mokṣa*'. So, generally speaking, *Mokṣa* has been regarded in India as the motivation for moral effort. *Mokṣa* has been taken as the highest *puruṣārtha* and morality or *dharma* has been generally taken as a means to it. This *Mokṣa* is a motivation not only for individual moral acts, but also for following moral principles and as a matter of fact for adopting the moral way of life itself.

It should be made clear that *Mokṣa* provides only a motive force for *dharma* or morality, and not a (rational) justification thereof. For, it does not provide the reason for being moral, it does not provide the answer to the question: 'What is the reason which justifies being moral?' But can *Mokṣa* prove to be even a motivation for *dharma* or morality? The question is relevant because only that can serve as a motivation for something which is more attractive, more valuable than the latter. Is *Mokṣa* more attractive and more valuable than *dharma*? We have discussed in an earlier chapter that Indian systems differ as to the exact nature of *Mokṣa*, but agree on some general points. Or we can say, in other words, that although Indian systems differ among themselves in details about the nature of *Mokṣa*, there is nearly a consensus on certain general points. They are: *Mokṣa* is a state of eternal peace, tranquillity and bliss, it is an end for ever of all suffering and pain, it is sometimes eternal abode in nearness to God, etc.

Descriptions of the state of *Mokṣa* in different systems unmistakably show that *Mokṣa* is an ontological status admitting of some description. Is the state of eternal peace and tranquillity more attractive than an active life of *dharma*? Perhaps not, at least not always. Peace and tranquillity have their attraction only in the midst of turmoil; bliss has its attraction only in the midst of suffering. If one is condemned to stay in eternal peace and bliss, that will not perhaps be a very attractive status for him. He will feel like leading a dull life and will be bored. Eternity hardly brings forth any glamour. Everything eternal is not attractive. Eternal or absolute bliss may not be eternal or absolute good too.

Even as a value *Mokṣa* is not necessarily higher than *dharma*. Why is *Mokṣa* higher than *dharma*? Perhaps reply to this question will be no other than 'because it is the highest value, the ultimate value'. But the question still remains where it was: 'why is *Mokṣa* to be regarded as the highest or ultimate value?, 'Why not *dharma* itself be regarded as the ultimate value?' The answer will again perhaps centre round the point that *Mokṣa* gives eternal bliss which *dharma* is not able to give. But what gives permanent bliss is not necessarily to be regarded on that account as more desirable or something higher. It seems to be a mere dogma to regard *Mokṣa* as the end and *dharma* as a means. Between the end and the means the former is rated higher than the latter. But it is not always justified to think that the end is higher than the means. Gandhi has always emphasized equal, almost identical, status for both the means and the end. Moreover, if there is a need for justification (in the sense of motivation) of *dharma*, why not the same for *Mokṣa* also? It is quite dogmatic to assert that *Mokṣa* is the highest value.

Now, let us see the answer to the question of justification in the second sense, i.e., in the sense of giving reason. We have said it earlier that no question regarding the rational justification of morality has been raised or attempted to be answered on the conscious level in the Indian ethical thought. Even if we raise a question here and seek an answer thereto, we can find the answer for the most part contained in authority. But a justification based on authority is no justification perhaps, because very meaningfully one can seek for the justification of the justifying authority itself. We have already seen that there is hardly any scope for justification by reason in Indian ethics. So justification of any moral act or principle by way of deducing it from higher principle or principles is out of question. And if it is the case with individual acts and principles, one can very well realise that there can be no question of justifying the institution of morality with reference to any deductive reasoning. Instead of leaving any scope for deductive justification of morality, Indian thinkers have sometimes exhibited an allergical attitude, rather, towards seeking any rational or inferential justification of *dharma*. We have seen (in Chapter II) the Mīmāṃsakas, specially the Prabhākaras, asserting that *dharma* does not require any rational or logical support. It justifies itself. They are so conscious about the irrelevance or absurdity of justification of *dharma* that they take specific care in interpreting *arthavāda* passages as passages of praise and commendation of *dhārmika* practices, although they look like advancing reason for them.

However, in the other sense of giving reason or advancing rational justification for morality, there is ample scope in the Indian system for developing a justification for morality. Even in this sense, of course, there has been no conscious effort to advance any justification for *dharma*, for, as we have said repeatedly, no need was ever felt by the Indian thinkers to advance any rational justification of morality, because morality in their view was based primarily on Śāstras and the Śāstras did not require any justification. One is required to have absolute faith in them, and there is no scope for any doubt or discussion. But there are elements in Indian thought which advance full justification for the individual moral acts as well as for the moral way of life.

The general conception of man, for example, that is there in Indian philosophy is itself a sufficient ground or justification for morality. Every man has got a soul as his essence within him, which, if not the same, is at least similar. In what constitutes man's essential life, all men are alike. In the Vedāntic doctrine '*tat tvam asi*', identity of essence rather than mere similarity is emphasized, and in it lies perfect justification for man's adopting a life of morality. If all men are essentially one, there is naturally a full justification for adopting a life of love, compassion, mutual help etc. which are the essential ingredients of social morality. In the self-same principle, there lies the element of individual morality also. Because man is not simply a body along with its sense-organs, rather in his essential being he is a higher spiritual reality, a soul which endures all change and destruction, he should therefore adore the latter and not the former. With control of the senses (*indriyanigraha*) man is advised to lift himself higher towards spiritual life. For this, winning over the passions, purifying the mind (*cittaśuddhi*) etc. become essential elements of individual morality. Thus similarity or identity of essence proves to be an ample justification for man to adopt a moral way of life. From the former, of course, the latter does not follow deductively, but accepting the former as a true belief quite reasonably leads one to the latter, much in the same way in which 'one should not build houses on this river bank' does not necessarily follow from the premise that 'There is severe flood in the river every year', but it is still rational to accept the former if one accepts the latter as true.

In the Indian context, man's own nature furnishes a justification for his being moral. Perhaps this is why most Indian systems prove to be deontological in nature. According to them, *dharma* is to be followed because it is its own justification. *Mokṣa* has been brought forth as a motivation in the sense that one who will follow *dharma* will automatically pave his way for that, but *Mokṣa* has never been taken as a justification for being moral. Morality is involved in the nature of man. It is in view of this essentially spiritual nature of man that the *Kaṭhopaniṣad* distinguishes between *sreyaḥ* and *preyaḥ* and counsels that it is the former, and not the latter, which ought to be pursued by man. In other words, it says that it is the former, and not the latter, which is up to the nature of man. And the former is the course of virtue or morality.

In Rāmānuja, one can find the justification of morality in a different manner. Rāmānuja believes that God, the Supreme Lord, the creator, sustainer of the world, is also its inner moral governor. God, according to him, is full of moral excellences. Now, because God, the Lord, is full of moral excellences, so man, his creature, also should be so. It is the duty of man as man to follow God by observing the moral qualities that he possesses in him as paradigms. According to Rāmānuja, the greatest devotion of man to God lies in the former's following the path of morality, the path which the moral qualities of God point to. In Rāmānuja's view, man in one sense is the co-partner of God. He, therefore, has to follow God's mission of attaining the goal of Absolute God. In other words, being the co-partner of God, man is the follow the path of morality. So man's being moral finds full justification in the sense that when God, his creator and sustainer, is himself full of moral virtues and wants that his fellow-creatures should imitate him in this respect, it is the duty of man to be moral.

The kind of justification sought for morality in the Indian context may very well lead one to remark that it is not proper to have sought to justify morality on the basis of metaphysics. Metaphysics or metaphysical beliefs cannot furnish a justification for morality because no ought—sentence can be derived from is—sentence. If we try to do so, we become a victim of naturalistic fallacy. But here we should mark that we have not tried to justify morality on the basis of metaphysics in the sense of deriving the former from the latter. It is not a fact that morality has been deduced out of some metaphysics or metaphysical belief. It has been simply pointed out that with some metaphysical beliefs being taken as true, certain moral principles or even a whole moral way of life can be reasonably accepted. So, there is no question of fallacy like that of the Naturalistic one, even if the so-called thesis of the non-derivability of 'ought' out of 'is' is accepted as true.

The above seems to be an attempt for establishing the position that in some sense of giving reason for morality, there are certain metaphysical beliefs involved in the Indian tradition which advance reason for being moral and thus there is scope for justifying the moral way of life in the Indian tradition. But one may very reasonably ask here, why accept those metaphysical beliefs themselves? Why believe, for example, that there is a soul which is so and so or that there is a God who is so and so? Of course, there are proofs for both in the Indain tradition and there is also the plea that it is on the basis of direct intuitive experience that we know such metaphysical beliefs as true. But it is quite clear that none of these can stand the test of logical scrutiny. However we have to say against such protests, and perhaps rightly, that they are the very basic presuppositions from which Indian thought flows. If these presuppositions are questioned, the whole structure of Indian thought will fall into pieces and there will be nothing with reference to which we can say that we are taking things in the Indian context. So these presuppositions are not to be questioned at all. When we raise the question of the justification of morality in the Indian context, we raise it in the existing Indian context which include all the fundamental beliefs and presuppositions which give it its own distinctive nature.

REFERENCES

1. R.L. Stevenson, *Ethics and Language* (Yale Univ. Press, 1994), p. 27 ff., 138 ff.
2. R.M. Hare, *The Language of Morals* (Oxford Univ. Press, 1952) Part I, Sec. 3. Also, *Freedom and Reason* (Oxford Paperback, 1965), Part II.
3. P.H. Nowell-Smith, *Ethics* (Penguin Books Ltd., 1954), p. 80 ff.
4. F.H. Bradley, *Ethical Studies*, (Oxford Univ. Press, 1962), p. 58.
5. R.M. Hare, *The Language of Morals*, Part I, Sec. 4, P.H. Nowell-Smith, *op. cit.*, p. 308 ff.
6. R.M. Hare, *Freedom and Reason*, 86 ff.

Selected Bibliography

CLASSICAL TEXTS

The Vedas and the Upaniṣads, Sacred Books of the East Series (Motilal Banarsidass, Delhi), Vols. I, IV, XXXII, XLVI.

Ṛg Veda, tr. R.T.H. Griffith (Chowkhamba, Banaras).

Atharva Veda, tr. R.T.H. Griffith (E.J. Lazarus and Co., Banaras).

Eleven Principal Upaniṣads (Gita Press, Gorakhpur).

Śatapatha Brāhmaṇa, ed. A Weber, tr. J. Eggeling (London, 1885).

Manusmṛti (Chowkhamba Sanskrit Series, Banaras, 1979).

Laws of Manu, tr. G. Bühler, Sacred Books of the East Series, Vol. XXV (Motilal Banarsidass, 1979).

Āpastamba Dharmasūtra (Chowkhamba Sanskrit Series, Banaras, 1969).

Gautama Dharmasūtra (Chowkhamba Sanskrit Series, Banaras, 1966).

Yājñavalkya Smṛti (Chowkhamba Sanskrit Series, Banaras, 1977).

Mīmāṃsā Sūtras of Jaiminī, tr. Ganganath Jha (Sacred Books of the Hindus Series, Vol. X, Part I, ed. B.D. Basu (Panini Office, Allahabad).

Sabara-Bhāṣya, Eng. tr. Ganganath. Jha.

Śloka Vārtika of Kumārila Bhaṭṭa, Eng. tr. Ganganath Jha.

Tantravārtika of Kumārila Bhaṭṭa, Eng. tr. Ganganath Jha.

Gautama's Nyāya-Sūtras with Vātsyāyana's Bhāṣya, tr. Ganganath Jha (Poona Oriental Series).

Padārthadharmasaṃgraha of Prasastapāda with the Nyāya-Kandali of Śrīdhara, Eng. tr. Ganganath Jha (E.J. Lazarus and Co., Banaras).

The Sāṃkhya Aphorisms of Kapila, tr. J.R. Ballantyne.

Sāṃkhya Pravacana Bhāṣya of Vijñānabhikṣu (Chowkhamba, Banaras).

Patañjali's Yoga-Sūtras with the commentaries of Vyāsa and the gloss of Vācaspati Miśra, Eng. tr. Rama Prasad, Sacred Books of the Hindu Series, ed. B.D. Basu (Panini Office, Allahabad).

The Yoga System of Patañjali, tr. J.H. Woods (Harvard Oriental Series, Vol. 17).

Vedānta Sūtras with the commentaries of Śaṃkara, Eng. tr. George Thibaut, Sacred Books of the East Series (Motilal Banarsidass),

Vol. XXXIV.
Vedānta Sūtras with the commentaries of Rāmānuja, tr. George Thibaut, S.B.E., Vol. XLVIII.

OTHER BOOKS

Aiyangar, K.V. Rangaswami, *Some Aspects of the Hindu View of Life According to Dharmaśāstra* (Baroda Oriental Institute, 1952).
Aiyer, P.S., *Evolution of Hindu Ethical Ideals* (Calcutta, University, 1935).
Aurobindo, Sri, *The Human Cycle* (Pondicherry, 1962).
Baier, Kurt, *The Moral Point of View* (New York, Random House, 1965).
Bloomfield, *Religion of the Vedas* (Indological Book House, Delhi, 1972).
Bradley, F.H., *Ethical Studies* (Oxford, 1962).
Buch, M.A., *The Principles of Hindu Ethics* (Hathi Pole Baroda, 1921).
Dasgupta, Surama, *Development of Moral Philosophy in India* (Orient Longmans, 1961).
Deussen, Paul, *The System of Vedānta* (Chicago Open Court, 1912).
Falk, W.D., Morality, Self and Others' included in Pahel and Schiller's (ed.), *Readings in Contemporary Ethical Theory* (Prentice Hall, New Jersey, 1970).
Frankena, W.K., 'The Concept of Morality' included in Pahel and Schiller's (ed.), *op. cit.*
Frankena, W.K., *Ethics* (Prentice Hall, New Jersey, 1975).
Ganguli, K.M. (ed.), *The Mahābhārata* (Munshiram Manoharlal, New Delhi, 1974).
Hare, R.M., *The Language of Morals* (Oxford, 1952).
Hare, R.M., *Freedom and Reason* (Oxford Paperback, 1965).
Hiriyanna, M., *Essentials of Indian Philosophy.*
Hopkins, E.W., *Ethics of India* (New Haven, Yale University Press, 1924).
Jha, Ganganath, *Pūrva Mīmāṃsā in its Sources* (B.H.U., 1964 ed.).
Keith, A.S., *Religion and Philosophy of the Veda and Upaniṣads* (Indian Repr. Motilal Banarsidass, 1970).
Lefever, H., *The Vedic Idea of Sin* (London Mission Press, Nagarcoil, Travancore, 1935).
Maitra, S.K., *Ethics of the Hindus* (Calcutta, University, 1963).
Mckenzie, John, *Hindu Ethics* (Oriental Book Reprint Corporation, New Delhi, 1971).
Mishra, Brahmashankar, *Sukra Nitisāra* (Chowkhamba, 1968).
Miśra, Pārthasārthī, *Śāstradīpikā* (Baroda Oriental Institute, 1940).

Nowell-Smith, P.H., *Ethics* (Penguin Books, 1954).
Radhakrishnan, S., *The Bhagavadgītā* (Allen and Unwin, London, 1948).
Radhakrishnan, S., *Eastern Religions and Western Thought,* (Oxford, 1940).
Radhakrishnan, S., *The Vedānta* (Allen and Unwin, 1928).
Radhakrishnan, S., *Indian Philosophy,* 2 Vols.
Radhakrishnan, S., *An Idealist View of Life* (Allen and Unwin, 1932).
Stephen, Leslie, *The Sciences of Ethics* (New York, 1882).
Stevenson, R.L., *Ethics and Language* (Yale University Press, 1946).
Tachibana, S., *The Ethics of Buddhism* (London, Curzon Press, 1926).
Tagore, R.N., *The Religion of Man* (Allen and Unwin, London, 1949).
Tagore, R.N., *Sadhana* (Macmillan, London, 1964).
Tilak, B.G., *Gītarahasya* (Hindi Edition), (Poona, 1964).
Warnock, G.J., *The Object of Morality* (Metheun and Co. Ltd. London, 1971).

Index